Contents

Acknowledgements

Thanks are due to many people who helped with the compilation of this guide. I owe a debt to many colleagues who have shared my enthusiasm for the Victorian censuses and who have sat behind the census room enquiry desk at one time or another: Joe Saunders, who taught me all I know; Andy Bodle, Nigel Kent and Gerry Toop, who contributed helpful advice; Amanda Bevan, Mandy Banton, John Post, David Crook, Elizabeth Hallam Smith, Alfred Knightbridge and Sheila Knight, who guided a rough draft through many editorial metamorphoses to its present state; Evelyn Goode, who did an enormous amount of work essential to the revamping of the finding aids, and Melvyn Stainton, who helped with the finding aids and also drew the illustrations for the book; Hugh Ashley Rayner, who photographed the documents; Margaret Brennand for explaining the digitised census and how it is accessed; Dave Annal who advised on updating the material on the FRC; and especially Edward Higgs, whose much greater knowledge of how and why the census was taken was always there to be tapped when necessary. Thanks are also due to the late Alan Reed who provided some useful information based on his considerable experience as a lecturer on the subject and, last but not least, to all those searchers, record agents and transcribers who pointed out interesting entries, who shared their experience and who asked the questions.

Making Use *of the* Census

Fourth revised edition

Susan Lumas

PUBLIC RECORD OFFICE

Public Record Office Readers' Guide No. 1

First edition published by the Public Record Office in 1992
Fourth edition first published in 2002 by

Public Record Office
Kew
Richmond
Surrey
TW9 4DU

www.pro.gov.uk/

Front and back cover: household servants at Squerreys Lodge, Westerham, Kent, by Arthur Thomas Dean (PRO COPY 1/408). Other photographs can be seen on pp. 8 and 67 of the text.

Publisher's note: all census transcripts within the text are reproduced as written by the enumerator.

Printed in Great Britain by Antony Rowe, Chippenham, Wiltshire

Illustrations

Introduction

The purpose of this guide is to help researchers to find their way into the nineteenth-century census returns held by the Public Record Office (PRO). Whether they are seeking to compare occupations in a particular suburb of an industrial town over a thirty-year period, or to search for an individual in the course of piecing together a family history, it will guide them in understanding and interpreting this significant and fascinating source. It explains how to cope with the census reading rooms at the Family Records Centre (FRC), and how to use the PRO's finding aids to identify the relevant microfilm, the medium by which the records are made available for 1841–91. (The 1881 census is also available in transcript format on fiche or on CD-ROM, and the 1901 census is available on fiche and online (see pp. 49–53).) The guide should be of value to those consulting the copies of census returns held outside the PRO in local record offices and libraries, because it clarifies the structure of the census and also deals with a variety of problems encountered by its readers (e.g. how to locate a particular place or seek a missing house).

Making use of the census

The nineteenth-century census returns provide a fascinating field of study and a valuable introduction to the use of archives. Many people do not think of consulting the census returns until their studies require them to provide a detailed background to their area of research, be that general population studies of an economic or social nature, through research into particular localities, to studies of individuals by family historians and biographers. It is not possible, however, just to walk into a reading room to find an index designed for your exact purpose that will lead you straight to the required page or pages of the census returns. Archives are left in the order in which they remained after their immediate administrative use was over, which tells us something of how they were compiled and administered. They have not been rearranged to suit the potential user, because today's researcher may not be seeking the same information as a reader of one hundred years hence.

Joseph Cash, Manufacturer of Silk and Cotton (RG 10/3182, ff. 39–40)

The ideal enumerator
'A person of intelligence and activity, he must read and write well and have some knowledge of arithmetic. He must not be infirm or of such weak health as may render him unable to undergo the requisite exertion. He should not be younger than 18 years or older than 65 years. He must be temperate, orderly and respectable and be such a person as is likely to conduct himself with strict propriety and deserve the good will of the inhabitants of his district.'

The ideal householder
'The schedule should be received with intelligent acquiescence, and filled up with the persuasion that the integrity and enlightenment of all are tacitly challenged to take a conscientious share fulfilling a truly important duty.'

The Caernarfon and Denbigh Herald, 1871

Walter Palmer, Biscuit Manufacturer (RG 12/992, f. 138)

What there is and where to find it

A census of Great Britain has been taken every decade from 1801 onwards, with the exception of 1941 when war intervened. The results were digested and published as Parliamentary Papers, to provide population counts (see Appendix 1) and other social statistics for immediate use. For a detailed study of how and why the census was taken see Higgs, *Making Sense of the Census* and *A Clearer Sense of the Census* (see Bibliography).

The earlier returns for 1801 to 1831 were simply a numerical count, and give little detailed information except where an enumerator decided to exceed his duties and include more. These returns have not been officially preserved, but some survive locally, often in county record offices. The whereabouts of such survivals may be discovered by consulting Gibson's *Marriage, Census and other Indexes for Family Historians*, and Chapman's *Pre 1841 Censuses and Population Listings*.

From 1841, however, all the enumerators' returns (but not the original schedules) have been officially preserved, in theory, although in practice not all have survived. It was realised that these returns could usefully serve purposes other than those intended by the original survey.

All the returns for England and Wales, which include the Isle of Man and the Channel Islands (referred to as Islands in the British Seas), the Isle of Wight (returned with Hampshire), and the Scilly Isles (returned with Cornwall), for 1841 to 1901 (HO 107, RG 9 to RG 13) are available on microfilm, and also on microfiche for 1881–1901.

Access to census returns

For some time now census returns have only been available on microfilm. The original documents are produced only rarely when they are impossible to read on film, and this, of course, can only be done at the PRO reading rooms at Kew.

More recently, the 1891 documents have also been available on fiche, as are the 1901 documents at Kew.

The 1881 documents are not available in the original format on fiche, but there is a transcript available on fiche and CD-ROM. At the FRC, the 1881 census is uniquely available on networked computer with other family history databases, meaning that you don't have to use separate CD-ROM disks.

HM Napoleon III, Emperor of the French (RG 10 / 876, ff. 13–14, 46, p. 82)

In 2002, the 1901 digitised census appeared online worldwide (at www. census.pro.gov.uk), and in future more censuses will become available this way.

This means you have various choices, depending on where you are viewing the documents. The grid below shows what forms of access are now available at the FRC and at Kew, and indicates the type of access available elsewhere depending on what has been obtained by other venues for research.

Year	Originals				Transcripts		
	Film	Fiche	CD-ROM	Online	Fiche	CD-ROM	Online
1841	✓ *						
1851	✓ *						
1861	✓ *						
1871	✓ *						
1881	✓ *				✓	✓ +	
1891	✓ *	✓	London, with more to follow				
1901	✓	✓ **		✓ †			✓ †

*   available in this form at the FRC census searchroom
** available at the PRO, Kew
†   available at the FRC and the PRO, Kew
+   available at the FRC as a networked computer database

Where to go

The returns for the whole of England and Wales can be viewed in central London at the FRC. At the PRO, Kew, you can view the 1901 only, either online or on fiche.

Family Records Centre
1 Myddelton Street
London EC1R 1UW
Telephone: 020 8392 5300
Fax: 020 8392 5307
Internet: www.familyrecords.gov.uk/frc

Public Record Office
Kew, Richmond
Surrey TW9 4DU
Telephone: 020 8876 3444
Fax: 020 8878 8905
Internet: www.pro.gov.uk/

John Cadbury, Cocoa Manufacturer (RG 9/2124, ff. 4–5, pp. 1–3)

Monday, Wednesday, Friday	9 a.m. to 5 p.m.
Tuesday	10 a.m. to 7 p.m.
Thursday	9 a.m. to 7 p.m.
Saturday	9.30 a.m. to 5 p.m.

Individual areas in various formats will be found in some county record offices and local studies libraries (see Gibson's *Census Returns 1841–1891 in Microform*). In the United States of America, all census returns can be accessed at the Family History Library, 50 East North Temple, Salt Lake City, Utah 84150.

The returns are, however, subject to a one hundred year closure period because of the personal information which they contain. One hundred years means one hundred years, not ninety-nine years and a half; the census returns, having usually been taken in April, are opened after their closure period on the first working day of the following year. For the dates of census night for each year see Appendix 1.

The 1911 census for England and Wales is still in the custody of the Registrar General. Because of the stricter assurances of confidentiality given at that time than for earlier censuses it is not possible to consult it for information in advance of its opening date in 2012. Also, the returns for that year were not entered into enumerators' books, so a search of the original schedules which are retained in place of the books would present considerable difficulties.

The Scottish returns are held at the General Register Office for Scotland, New Register House, Edinburgh EH1 3YT (telephone 0131 334 0380). The 1881, 1891 and 1901 returns are available online at www.gro-scotland.gov.uk.

Irish returns rarely survive before 1901. *Handbook on Irish Genealogy*, published by Heraldic Artists Ltd., Dublin, lists on p. 39 those census records which have survived in the National Archives in Dublin for some counties. Begley's *Irish Genealogy: A Record Finder* (p. 51), has a comprehensive survey of Irish census returns from as far back as 1630 and up to 1981, and a full list of what has survived. These two lists are not identical.

Censuses were also taken in many British colonies on the same dates as those for the UK, but little information other than the purely statistical exists for them in this country. There is, however, a census of convicts in New South Wales and Tasmania, 1788 to 1859, in HO 10/21–27; an 1811 census of Surinam (CO 278/15–25); a 1715 census of Barbados but only of the white population (CO 28/16); and a census of Sierra Leone for 1831 (CO 267/111).

Arrangement of the records

The census returns are arranged topographically (that is, by place) in the order in which they appear in the published tables. The arrangement follows the system used for the registration of births, marriages and deaths. In 1836, when civil registration was established, the poor law unions were used as a foundation for the boundaries of the registration districts. The superintendent registrars' districts, grouped into eleven divisions, were also used as administrative units for census taking and were numbered. The divisions are described in Appendix 2. The returns appear in numerical order of registration district. Later legislation altered the boundaries of the superintendent registrar's districts in order to confine individual districts within county boundaries which hitherto some had straddled. Some places, therefore, moved from one district to another as later censuses were taken. See Appendix 7 for a list of registration districts and their numbers.

Each superintendent registrar's district is divided into sub-districts, and each sub-district into enumeration districts. The enumeration districts vary in size. Those covering a rural area took into account the distance that one man could travel in a day to collect the schedules from each household. On the other hand, enumeration districts in large towns, with a greater concentration of people, cover a much smaller area on the ground but a much larger number of individuals. Parishes, townships, tithings, hamlets and liberties are gathered into appropriate enumeration districts, which may consist of several small places or an entire parish. In other cases there may be several enumeration districts covering one large parish. It is important to remember that these parishes are civil parishes and do not necessarily have the same boundaries as their ecclesiastical equivalents.

The civil parish was the result of poor law administration which in itself created boundary problems. The ecclesiastical parishes, which were based on the ancient parishes of England and Wales together with chapelries created when the population increased and needed more places of worship, were found to be too large and unwieldy for administrative purposes and individual townships or tithings and villages were allowed to levy their own rates. This resulted in the establishment of civil parishes, as distinct from ecclesiastical districts or parishes, especially during the nineteenth century. In 1871 the ancient parishes which had not already been sub-divided into chapelries and townships were renamed as civil parishes. In addition, there were extra-parochial places called liberties, or simply termed extra-parochial. All of these sub-divisions are mentioned in the population tables; the ecclesiastical districts are in separate sections at the end of each region. For census searching, however, ecclesiastical districts are usually ignored and the civil parish is the unit which matters.

John Poyntz, Earl and Groom to the Prince Consort (RG 9/949, f. 32, p. 19)

How the census was taken

In the week preceding census night (see Appendix 1 for the date of each census) the appointed enumerator delivered schedules (see pp. 8 and 9) to all the households in the area to which he had been assigned. The schedule was a form that every householder was obliged to complete. A householder was anyone who rented or owned a dwelling, a lodger being a householder if he or she lived in the same building but had separate accommodation from the rest of the people living there. A boarder was someone who lived with the householder's family and shared their dining table, unlike a lodger who occupied a separate household (see p. 65 for a boarder and a lodger under one roof). Everyone who slept in the house on census night was to be included, even if it was not their permanent home. The instructions to the enumerator were that no person present on that night was to be omitted, and no person absent included. If individuals were working that night, or were travelling, they would be enumerated in the house to which they would normally return on the morning after they had finished their shift, or where they were to stay at the next stop on their journey.

ENUMERATOR'S REMARKS FROM 1851 CENSUS FOR LONDON
ALL HALLOWS, BARKING, LONDON

The enumeration of this district was undertaken by me in the belief that I should be fairly paid for my services.

I was not aware that all the particulars were to be entered by the enumerator in a book, the work without that, being ample for the sum paid, nor had I any idea of the unreasonable amount of labour imposed. The distribution, collection etc of the schedules together with the copying of the same occupied from two or three hours for every sixty persons enumerated, and for that – the equivalent is – ONE SHILLING!!!

What man possessing the intelligence and business habits necessary for the undertaking would be found to accept it, if aware of the labour involved. How then can a correct return of the population be expected?

He who proposed the scale of remuneration, should, in justice, be compelled to enumerate a large district, such as this upon the terms he had himself fixed.

HO 107 / 1531, f. 193

Henry Mackeson, Alderman Brewer (HO 107 / 1633, f. 543, p. 1)

CENSUS OF ENGLAND AND WALES, 1871.

No. 196

HOUSEHOLDER'S SCHEDULE.

Prepared under the direction of one of Her Majesty's Principal Secretaries of State, pursuant to the Act of 33d and 34 Vict., c. 107.

Parish or Township	Sheffield
City, Town, &c.	Sheffield
Street, Square, &c., or Road	Victoria Street
Name or No. of House	37
Name of Occupier	Wrangham

TO THE OCCUPIER.

You are requested to insert the particulars specified on the other side, in compliance with an Act which passed the House of Commons, and the House of Lords, in the last Session of Parliament, and received the assent of Her Majesty The Queen on the 10th of August, 1870.

This Paper will be CALLED FOR on MONDAY, APRIL 3rd, by the appointed Enumerator,

and it is desirable that you should have the answers written in the proper columns by the *morning of that day*, in order that his progress may not be delayed. It will be his duty, under the Act, to complete the return if it be defective, and to correct it if erroneous. Any person authorized by you may write in the particulars if you are yourself unable to do so.

Persons who refuse to give correct information, are liable to a *Penalty of Five Pounds*; besides the inconvenience and annoyance of appearing before two Justices of the Peace, and being convicted of having made a wilful mis-statement of age, or of any of the other particulars.

The Return is required to enable the Secretary of State to complete the RETURN (CENSUS); which is to show the exact numbers, ages, and condition of the people—their arrangement by families in different ranks, professions, and trades—their distribution over the country in villages, towns, and cities—their increase and progress during the last ten years. The facts will be published in General Abstracts only, and strict care will be taken that the return are not used for the gratification of curiosity.

GEORGE GRAHAM,
Registrar General.

Approved.
H. A. BRUCE,
Home Office, Whitehall, Nov. 17th, 1870.

GENERAL INSTRUCTION.

This Paper to be filled up by the OCCUPIER or person in charge of the dwelling.

If a house is let or sub-let to separate Families or Lodgers, each OCCUPIER or LODGER must make a return for his portion of the house upon a SEPARATE PAPER.

INSTRUCTIONS for filling up the Column headed "RANK, PROFESSION, or OCCUPATION."

A person following more Distinct Occupations than one, should insert them in the order of their importance.

1. The superior Titles of PEERS and other PERSONS OF RANK to be inserted; as also must every member of both HOUSES OF PARLIAMENT.

2. MEMBERS of important public Offices, to state their profession or occupation, if any, after their official rank or title.

3. All persons serving in the ARMY AND NAVY, to state their rank and whether on the Active or Retired List; Chelsea, Greenwich, and other Pensioners, to be so designated.

4. All persons in the CIVIL SERVICE to state their rank, and the department or branch to which they belong; those retired or superannuated to be distinguished.

5. MINISTERS OF RELIGION.—Clergymen of the Church of England to return themselves as "*Rector of* —," "*Vicar of* —," "*Curate of* —," "&c., or "*without cure of souls*;" They are requested not to employ the indefinite term "*Clerk*." Roman Catholic Priests, and Ministers of Foreign Churches, to return themselves as such, and to state the name of the church or chapel in which they officiate. Dissenting Ministers to return themselves as "*Independent Minister of* — *Chapel*," or "*Wesleyan Methodist preacher*," &c., &c.

6. LEGAL PROFESSION.—Barristers to state whether or not they are in actual practice. The designation *Attorney, Solicitor, Proctor,* &c., are to be used as they actually are in Solicitors' Offices should state whether they are *Solicitors' Managing, Articled,* or *General Clerk*. Officers of any Court, to state the name of the Office, and the nature of the Court.

7. Members of the MEDICAL PROFESSION to state whether they practise as *Physician, Surgeon, Dentist, Oculist, General Practitioner, Assistant,* &c., or are "not practising." They must also state the University or other Society of which they are Graduates, Fellows, or Licentiates.

8. PROFESSORS, TEACHERS, PUBLIC WRITERS, Authors and Scientific men—to state the particular branch of Science of Literature which they follow; Artists, the art which they cultivate. Graduates should enter their degrees in this column.

9. STUDENTS of *Theology, Law,* or *Medicine*, and *Under-graduates* of any University, to be so returned.

10. SCHOLARS.—Children or young persons attending a School, or receiving regular instruction at home, to be returned as *Scholars*. Against the name of a Child above five years of age, in Wales, being Agricultural land, pastures, moor, or woodland, in addition to their rank or occupation, to state that they are *landowners*. But no person to be so described in respect of land attached to a house or garden, not exceeding one acre in extent.

11. FARMERS to state the number of acres, and the number of men, women, and boys, employed on the farm on April 3rd.—*Examples:* "*Farmer of 317 Acres, employing 8 Labourers and 3 Boys.* Sons or Daughters employed on the farm, may be returned—"*Farmer's Son,*" "*Farmer's Daughter.*" Men employed on the farm and sleeping in the Farmer's house must be described in the schedule as *Farm Servants*.

13. AGRICULTURAL LABORERS, SHEPHERDS, and others employed on Farms, but not living in the Farmer's house, must be described as *Agricultural Labourers, Shepherds,* &c.

14. PERSONS ENGAGED IN COMMERCE as Merchants, Brokers, Agents, &c., to state in all cases the particular branch of Commerce in which they are engaged, or the staple in which they chiefly deal—*Examples:* "*East India Merchant*," "*Member of Stock Exchange*," "*Cotton Broker*."

COMMERCIAL CLERK, COMMERCIAL TRAVELLER, SHOPMAN—alway to add in what branch of business.

15. In TRADES, MANUFACTURES, or other Business, Masters must, in all cases, be distinguished.—*Example:* "*Carpenter—Master employing 6 men and 2 boys,*" inserting always the number of workpeople in their employ, if any, on April 3rd. In the case of Farms, the number of persons employed should be returned by the senior or some one partner only.

16. WORKERS in MANUFACTURES or MINES, and generally in the Mechanical Arts, should distinctly state the particular article made or material worked, and kind of work done in the manufacture, as in *Coal-miner, Brass-founder, Silk-throwster,* &c. Where the trade is much sub-divided, both trade and branch are to be returned thus—*Watchmaker—Finisher*; *Printer—Compositor*.

17. ENGINEERS.—Civil Engineers are to be distinctly described.—*Examples:* "*Engine Smith at Factory,*" "*Engine Fitter at Works.*" Engine Drivers, Stokers, and Firemen, to be described in connexion with the machinery, thus—"*Railway Engine Driver,*" "*Stoker in Cotton Factory,*" "*Engineer*" alone is not to be used.

18. ARTISANS and MECHANICS should invariably state the particular branch of mechanical art or business in which they are employed.

19. WEAVER—*Silk*," "*Wool*," "*Worsted*," "*Cotton,*" &c., should always be written before this general term, so as to express distinctly the material which he weaves, thus—*Silk Weaver*. Labourers are to be distinctly described according to the article in connexion with which they work, thus—"*Railway Porter,*" "*Bricklayer's Labourer,*" "*Labourer in Iron Works.*"

20. DOMESTIC SERVANTS to be described in all cases "*Domestic Servant*," "*Coachman—Domestic Servant,*" "*Gardener—Domestic Servant.*"

21. MESSENGERS, PORTERS, LABORERS, to be described according to the nature of their employment on the day, thus—"*Railway Porter,*" "*Bricklayer's Labourer,*" "*Labourer in Iron Works.*"

22. Persons ordinarily engaged in some industry, but OUT OF EMPLOYMENT on April 3rd, should be so described, as "*Coalminer, unemployed.*"

23. PERSONS FOLLOWING NO PROFESSION, TRADE, OR CALLING and holding no public office, but deriving their incomes chiefly from houses, dividends, interest of money, annuities, &c., may describe themselves accordingly. The indefinite terms *Gentleman, Esquire,* are not to be used. Persons who have retired from business should be entered thus—*Retired Farmer,*" "*Retired Silk Mercer,*" &c.

24. WOMEN AND CHILDREN. The occupation of the who are regularly employed from home, or who follow any business at home, is to be distinctly recorded. See also instruction No. 10.

NOTE.—Example of the mode of filling up the Schedule are given in another part of this paper.

THREE EXAMPLES of the MODE OF FILLING UP THE HOUSEHOLDER'S SCHEDULE.

	Name and Surname.	Relation to Head of Family.	Condition.	Sex.	Age (last Birthday).	Rank, Profession, or Occupation.	Where Born.	If (1) Deaf-and-Dumb. (2) Blind. (3) Imbecile or Idiot. (4) Lunatic.
1	George Wood	Head of Family	Married	M.	48	Farmer (of 317 acres, employing 8 labourers and 3 boys)	Surrey, Godstone	
2	Maria Wood	Wife	Married	F.	44	Farmer's Wife	Scotland	
3	Alan Wood	Son	Unmarried	M.	20	Farmer's Son	Surrey, Godstone	
4	Flora Jane Wood	Daughter	Unmarried	F.	18	Scholar	Kent, Ramsgate	
5	Ellen Wood	Mother	Widow	F.	71	Annuitant	Canada	
6	Eliza Edwards	Servant	Unmarried	F.	24	General Servant (Domestic)	Middlesex, Paddington	
7	Ann Young	Servant	Unmarried	F.	22	Dairymaid	Surrey, Croydon	
8	Thomas Jones	Servant	Unmarried	M.	21	Farm Servant	Essex, Epping	Lunatic
1	Janet Cox	Head of Family	Widow	F.	49	Staymaker	Scotland	Blind from Small-pox.
2	William Cox	Son	Unmarried	M.	18	Basket-maker	Surrey, Lambeth	
3	Sophia Cox	Daughter	Unmarried	F.	24	Dressmaker	Middlesex, Poplar	
4	Alexander Cox	Grandson		M.	11 months		Middlesex, Shoreditch	
5	Margaret Cox	Mother-in-law	Widow	F.	72	Formerly Laundress	Ireland	
6	John Butler	Boarder	Widower	M.	42	Printer—Compositor	France (British Subject)	
1	Walter Johnson	Lodger	Unmarried	M.	23	Ship Carpenter	Durham, Sunderland	

BY AUTHORITY:—FORD and TILT, Long Acre, London, Printers to Her Majesty's Stationery Office.

Householder's schedule for Victoria Street, Sheffield (RG 10 / 4677, f. 76)

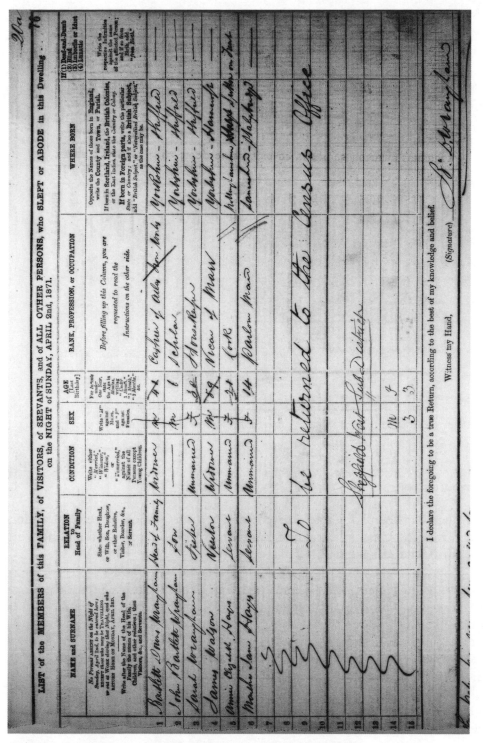

Completed schedule for the Wrangham family (RG 10/4677, f. 76)

On the Monday after the census night the enumerator returned to collect the completed schedules. If any had not been filled in, the enumerator had to do so by asking the householder for the information.

SUPERINTENDENT REGISTRAR'S DISTRICT.		Area in Statute Acres.	HOUSES.						POPULATION.			
			1851.			1861.			Persons.		Males.	
Sub-district.	Parish, Township, or Place.		Inha-bited.	Un-inha-bited.	Build-ing.	Inha-bited.	Un-inha-bited.	Build-ing.	1851.	1861.	1851.	1861.
495. TODMORDEN.												
1. HEBDEN BRIDGE	*Halifax, part of* Parish—ᵃ											
	Wadsworth - - Township	10080	957	166	–	923	158	2	4491	4141	2188	1995
	Erringden - - Township	2980	333	47	1	371	44	–	2004	1764	995	863
	Heptonstall - -ᵃᵃ Township	5320	882	127	2	790	170	6	4177	3497	2017	1728
	Stansfield, *part of* ᵃ -ᵃᵃ Township [viz., the Lower Third Division.]	5920	353	95	3	320	98	2	1790	1424	901	694
2. TODMORDEN -	*Halifax, part of* Parish—ᵃ											
	Stansfield, *part of* ᵃ - Township [viz., the Middle Third and Upper Third Division.]		1132	102	11	1351	62	16	5837	6750	2925	3286
	Langfield - - Township	2620	752	41	55	890	35	10	3729	4391	1805	2149
	Rochdale, part of Parish—ᵇ											
	TODMORDEN and Walsden (Lancashire) - -} Townp.	–	1481	114	31	1790	67	57	7699	9146	3738	4455
496. SADDLEWORTH.												
1. DELPH ᵇᵇ - -	Saddleworth, *part of* † - Township (*part of Rochdale* Parish.ᵇ) }		1819	230	10	2048	169	11	9440	9754	4647	4754
2. UPPER MILL ᵇᵇ	Saddleworth, *part of* (W) † - Township (*part of Rochdale* Parish.ᵇ) }	18280.	1548	105	18	1770	116	6	8359	8877	4190	4390
497. HUDDERSFIELD.												
1. SLAITHWAITE -	*Huddersfield, part of* Parish—ᶜ											
	Slaithwaite - - Township	2320	553	29	7	575	11	2	2852	2932	1460	1465
	Marsden { in *Huddersfield* Parish ᶜ -	2050	103	9	6	138	14	–	512	662	273	310
	Tnp.‡ ᵈ { in *Almondbury* Parish § -	5061	407	50	4	428	23	1	2153	2027	1091	1015
	Almondbury, part of Parish—§ ᵉ											
	Lingards - - Township	500	159	4	–	149	4	–	811	783	405	373
	Linthwaite, *part of* ‖ - ᶠ Township	809	264	13	–	309	16	2	1355	1567	692	789
2. MELTHAM - -	*Almondbury, part of* Parish—§ ᵉ											
	South Crosland - Township	1560	536	36	2	582	38	5	2784	2794	1392	1362
	Meltham - - Township	4525	684	42	10	795	75	2	3758	4046	1794	1885
3. HONLEY - -	*Almondbury, part of* Parish—§ ᵉ											
	Honley (W) - ᵍ Township	2790	1077	35	17	987	186	3	5595	4696	2775	2225
	Netherthong - Township	850	228	13	5	223	30	–	1207	1097	615	526
4. HOLMFIRTH -	*Almondbury, part of* Parish—§ ᵉ											
	Upperthong - ᵃᵃ Township	710	459	22	7	543	21	2	2463	2690	1235	1308
	Austonley - ᵉᵉ Township	1760	373	18	4	363	38	–	2234′	1901	1130	939
	Holme - - Township	3990	140	1	2	141	13	–	849	807	451	417
	Kirkburton, part of Parish—¶ ʰ											
	Cartworth, *part of* ** - ʲ Township	–	446	19	6	456	51	1	2298	2249	1168	1143
	Wooldale, *part of* †† - ʲ Township	–	657	36	11	668	54	–	3469	3198	1804	1624
5. NEWMILL - -	*Kirkburton, part of* Parish—¶ ʰ											
	Wooldale, *part of* †† - ʲ Township	2370	393	26	3	411	80	2	2131	2124	1070	1033
	Cartworth, *part of* ** - ʲ Township	2820	47	10	–	47	1	–	240	254	118	136
	Hepworth - - Township	3370	270	15	2	276	23	–	1532	1530	795	790
	Fulstone - - Township	1200	415	10	3	455	43	–	2257	2414	1177	1238

Population tables

The schedules were then copied by the enumerator into a book (several of which were bound together into folders) and handed in to the registrar who checked that everything was satisfactory.

The books were then sent to the census office in Craig's Court, London where they were checked again. Finally, when all the information had been analysed it was published as a Parliamentary Paper in the form of a series of tables relating to various subjects, and the original schedules were destroyed. The tables most used by searchers are the tables of population arranged by registration districts (see Bibliography). Copies are available at the FRC.

From 1891 women too could act as enumerators; it is not yet known how many accepted the challenge (see p. 64).

Gabriel Rossetti, Professor of Italian (HO 107/1493, f. 130, p. 13)

Using the census

Parts of the census may be viewed in one form or another in many venues; generally at a county record office or local history library. Each venue will have its own set of finding aids, either copies bought from the PRO or compiled locally. They will also have their own referencing system, in order to slot the films and fiche into their own holdings.

The following section explains the central London PRO reading rooms at the FRC, which hold all the returns for England and Wales. This will give you an idea of the range of material which can be used to identify a place, or indeed an individual, and will explain how you use standard types of finding aids in relation to the documents and means of access. Similar finding aids will be found elsewhere but systems, coverage and quality will vary.

At the FRC

On arrival at the Family Records Centre, Myddelton Street, if you ask to see the census records you will be directed to the reading room on the first floor. You do not need a reader's ticket.

You may leave your coat and excess baggage in the locker room on the lower ground floor before proceeding upstairs (£1 coin required, refundable). The FRC will not accept responsibility for loss or damage to personal property, so please watch any possessions taken in with you.

The lower ground floor also has plenty of space for eating and drinking when you need a break, and vending machines, but you will have to give up your seat to do this and acquire another seat number when you return to the reading room. There are facilities for disabled readers and a baby changing room.

The entrance area to the reading room has three desks on the left-hand side. The first one is dedicated to helping new visitors ('customers'). The second desk is the general enquiry desk, and the third is the copy service desk. Also in this area is a carousel of 'How to Use' leaflets.

The first thing you need to do before looking at a microfilm is to consult the books in the reference area. The finding aids provide you with all the information you need to identify the specific reels of film necessary for your search.

Thomas Boosey, Music Publisher (HO 107/662, book 4, f. 9, p. 9)

Before you help yourself to a microfilm you should obtain a dummy box with a seat number. These are located on shelving opposite the enquiry desks. The location of the blocks of seats is shown on the plan of the reading room on p. 83, and you will find the seat numbers on the tables in those areas. The box has to be returned whenever you leave the room and should replace the films you remove from the film drawers while you are using them.

Opposite the desks are the shelves containing the finding aids (reference books), which are grouped by census year and bound in different colours: 1841 in green, 1851 in red, 1861 in blue, 1871 in brown, 1881 in yellow and 1891 in black. They are described in greater detail from p. 13, but summarised here.

On the shelves, grouped by the years of the census, you will find:

• an index to places
• a series list which gives you the document references (also called a reference book)
• street indexes to London and other large towns
• copies of street directories for London
• a list of London streets and their whereabouts
• a list of the available surname indexes

On another set of shelves you will find copies of street directories for some places outside London. Also, between the finding aids for 1881 and 1891, you will find volumes which list abolished London street names (see 6(ii), p. 22) and ecclesiastical parishes (see 6(iv), p. 24).

Additionally, there are five volumes which help clarify the whereabouts of London streets and a volume that explains the changes in county boundaries and civil parishes during the nineteenth century. There is also an alphabetical index to registration districts which gives a list of churches and chapels in each.

The FRC also makes available, on microfiche and now on computer as part of *FamilySearch*, a copy of the *International Genealogical Index (IGI)* to enable people with an interest in individuals to ascertain in which county or counties a particular name is dominant. Once a successful search has been made for a family or an individual, a glance at the *IGI* will enlarge a searcher's knowledge of the spread of a particular surname in the county of birthplaces found in the census. It may even lead you to the specific reference in a parish or non-conformist register, as the *IGI* is an index to all the nonconformist registers held by the PRO and to many parish registers or parts of parish registers from all over the country.

William Wisden, Cricket Outfitter (RG 11/1088, f. 16, p. 25)

FamilySearch is a collection of databases holding genealogical information which includes the *International Genealogical Index* and *Ancestral File*, a database of genealogies sent in to the Church of Jesus Christ of Latter-day Saints by people throughout the world.

The section on finding aids which follows explains in more detail how to use the reference area. It is a self-service operation, although the staff are there to assist should you get into difficulties.

The cabinets holding the films are at the entrance to the part of the search room where you find the microfilm and microfiche readers.

In the area containing the microfilm readers there are reader-printers which enable you to obtain photocopies of successful searches from film or fiche. This is a self-service facility: see pp. 47 and 48, which shows you how to use a reader-printer, and p. 46 describing how to identify the particular part of the film you wish to copy.

Drinking, eating and the chewing of gum are forbidden in all parts of the census room. When you need a break, please eat and drink in the refreshment room provided on the lower ground floor. Smoking is forbidden throughout the building.

Using the reference area

To select a microfilm of the part of the census returns you wish to see, you need its reference number (see Appendix 4 for a full explanation of reference numbers). To determine this you need to look at one or more reference books, known as finding aids. The books are all clearly labelled by year and contents and are bound in different colours according to the year of the census (see p. 12). They are:

1 Place-name indexes
2 Series lists (reference books)
3 London street indexes
4 Country street indexes
5 A list of available surname indexes
6 Additional finding aids
   (i)   Index to London streets
   (ii) Index to abolished London street names
   (iii) Shipping index
   (iv) List of ecclesiastical parishes

Frederick Temple, Keeper of the Guildhall of the City of London (HO 107/1078, book 11, f. 29, p. 24)

    (v)   List of churches and chapels
    (vi) London street directories (also known as trade directories)
    (vii) Maps
    (viii)Population tables
    (ix) Miscellaneous topographical indexes

The census returns, as explained on p. 6, are arranged in numerical order of the superintendent registrars' districts. This presupposes that you know in which order they are numbered so that you can find your way around the country (see Appendixes 2 and 7). Once into your registration district you need to know which sub-district contains your place, and so on. Each set of census returns has an index to place names based on the index provided with the printed population tables. This is insufficient, however, when searching large towns, where it is totally impractical to read every frame on the film in the hope of finding the information you seek. Places with a population of over 40,000 have, therefore, been provided with a street index to take you to the correct folios of the enumerator's returns. These street indexes were produced by the PRO. Appendixes 8–13 list all the places covered for each census year.

To search the returns, therefore, you have three options at the outset. Your first port of call is to look at a place-name index. This will tell you whereabouts in the documents your place occurs and also whether there is a street index (see sections 3 and 4) which will shorten your search. If you are a family historian, you may find that there is a surname index for the place in which you have an interest, but you will need to know in which registration district if occurs. You will find a list of the surname indexes on the shelving in the reference area with the lists and indexes for each census year. If there is a surname index to help you, go straight to section 5, which will explain how to locate them and use them. If there is no surname index to your place or if you are not a family historian, read on.

1 Place-name indexes

The indexes of place names include the names of registration districts and of every other smaller division.

The index to places for 1841 gives you a page number to go to in the series list (see section 2). Place indexes for other years simply give you the name and number of the registration district in which that place occurs and, since the series lists are arranged in numerical order of registration district, it is a quick process to go from the place-name index to the series list in order to obtain the reference you need to identify your reel of film.

Benjamin Disraeli, Independent (HO 107/733, book 14, f. 45, p. 14)

PLACE NAME INDEX FOR 1841 CENSUS RETURNS

PLACE NAME	COUNTY ABBREV.	REF.BOOK PAGE NUMBER
Elmstead	Essex	90
Elmstead	Kent	144
Elmsthorpe	Leics	172
Elmstone	Kent	139
Elmstone Hardwicke	Glos	96,103
Elmstree	Glos	100
Elmton	Derb	52
Elm, Little	Som	303
Elm, North	Som	301
Elsdon	Northumb	249
Elsdon Ward	Northumb	249
Elsecar	Yorks WR	449
Elsenham	Essex	91
Elsey	Lincs	193
Elsfield	Oxon	269
Elsham	Lincs	187
Elsing	Norf	224
Elslack	Yorks WR	440
Elson	Salop	291
Elstead	Surrey	
Elsted	Sussex	
Elsthorpe	Lincs	
Elstob	Durh	
Elston	Lancs	
Elston	Notts	
Elston	Wilts	
Elstow	Beds	
Elstree	Herts	
Elstree	Midd	
Elstronwick	Yorks ER	
Elstub	Wilts	
Elswick	Lancs	
Elswick	Northumb	
Elsworth	Cambs	

Place-name index to 1841 returns

PLACE NAME INDEX FOR 1861 CENSUS RETURNS

PLACE NAME	COUNTY ABBREV	DISTRICT NAME	DIST NO.	SUB D.No	STREET INDEX	NAME INDEX
Bentley	Hants	Alton	114	2		
Bentley	Staffs	Walsall	380	1		
Bentley	Suff	Samford	221	2		
Bentley	Warw	Atherstone	397	1		
Bentley	Yorks ER	Beverley	518	2		
Bentley	Yorks WR	Doncaster	510	4		
Bentley Pauncefoot	Worcs	Bromsgrove	392	3		
Bentley, Great	Essex	Tendring	203	1		
Bentley, Little	Essex	Tendring	203	5		
Bentley, Lower	Worcs	Bromsgrove	392	3		
Bentley, Upper	Worcs	Bromsgrove	392	3		
Bentworth	Hants	Alton	114	1		
Benwell	Northumb	Newcastle upon Tyne	552	1	552	
Benwick	Cambs	North Witchford	191	1		
Beoley	Worcs	Kings Norton	393	1	393	
Bepton	Sussex	Midhurst	93	3		
Berden	Essex	Bishop Stortford	139	2		
Bere Regis	Dors	Wareham	273	4		
Bere Regis	Dors	Blandford	270	1		
Berechurch	Essex	Colchester	204	1		
Bergholt, East	Suff	Samford	221	1		
Bergholt, West	Essex	Lexdon	205	4		
Berkeley	Glos	Thornbury	332	3		
Berkeswell	Warw	Meriden	396	2		
Berkhampstead	Herts	Berkhampstead	147	1		
Berkhampstead St Mary	Herts	Berkhampstead	147	1		
Berkhampstead, Great	Herts	Berkhampstead	147	1		
Berkhampstead, Little	Herts	Hertford	142	2		

Place-name index to 1861 returns

2 Series lists (reference books)

If you find there is no surname or street index for the place you wish to search, consult the place-name index and make a note of the registration district number in the column by the side of your place which is highlighted in yellow. You should next look at the series list for the appropriate year to find how places are grouped together and to ascertain the order in which you can expect to find them on the microfilm. The series list is arranged in numerical order of registration district, so you need to discover the correct number before you look at the list.

In 1841 the census returns are grouped by hundreds, and in the northern counties, wapentakes, rather than by registration districts. From the place-name index you will be guided to the *page* of the series list where your place occurs.

In all other census years the place-name index will give you a registration district number. The series lists, arranged in numerical order of registration district, will show places grouped together by sub-district within each registration district.

Robert M Ballantyne, Literature (Chiefly Juvenile Fiction) (RG 11/1357, f. 9, p. 11)

Reference		HEREFORDSHIRE		HO 107
HO 107	HUNDRED	PARISH	TOWNSHIP	HAMLET
418	Broxash	Avenbury		
		Bodenham	Bodenham	
			Bowley	
			Bryan-Maund	
			Whitchurch-Maund	
			The Moor	
		Bredenbury		
		Bromyard	Brockhampton	
			(3)Linton	
			Norton	
			Winslow	
		Bockleton(part)*	Hampton-Charles	
		Collington		
		Little Cowarne		
		Much Cowarne		

			Llanveynoe
			Longtown
			Newton
		Cusop	
		Cwmyoy(part)*	Bwlch Trewyn
			Fwthog or Toothog
			Llancillo
		St Margaret's	
		Michael-Church-Eskley	
		Rowlstone	
		Walterstone	

HO 107/418	* Rest is in HO 107/1192
HO 107/419	* Rest is in HO 107/1194
HO 107/420	* Rest is in HO 107/742

- 122 -

89221 Dd 104657 30m 10/78

1841 series list

Each civil parish will include townships and hamlets, not all of which will necessarily be found in the same sub-district or registration district. A cross-referencing system in the footnotes to the series list will tell you where the rest of the parish may be found.

When you discover the exact place you want, the number in the reference column of the list, together with the group and series code in the box at the head of that column, is the full reference you need to identify your film. See Appendix 4 for a fuller explanation of the PRO referencing system.

Where a return does not survive the series list will show it as 'MISSING'.

Series lists also show you, by means of a bracketed number, the whereabouts of barracks, institutions and shipping. The key to these numbers is to be found in front of each series list and is as follows:

(1) barracks and military quarters
(2) HM ships at home
(3) workhouses (including pauper schools)
(4) hospitals (sick, convalescent, incurable)
(5) lunatic asylums (public and private)
(6) prisons
(7) certified reformatories and industrial schools
(8) merchant vessels
(9) schools

Arthur Chappell, Music Publisher (HO 107/1475, f. 410, p. 20)

3 London street indexes

If your search is in the returns for London you will certainly need a street index before you start to look in order to narrow your search. To attempt a search anywhere in London without such specific information is impractical; working through film after film on the off-chance of picking up one particular entry is a forlorn hope. The moment when you blink may be the moment the entry you want appears in the frame.

STREET INDEX TO THE 1861 CENSUS CLERKENWELL Street		THE PIECE NUMBER OF YOUR FILM	TO FIND YOUR PLACE ON THE FILM Folios
Warner Street, Great, Great Bath Street 1-30		RG9/194	81-81
	pt 16	RG9/194	100
Warner Street, Little, Roy Street		RG9/191	78-82
Warren Cottages, Warren Street		RG9/195	100-101
Warren Street, White Conduit Street	1-33	RG9/195	93-105
	2B & 3½	RG9/195	100
	14	RG9/195	105
	Warren Cottages	RG9/195	100-101
Waterloo Place, Clerkenwell Close		RG9/191	12-16
Wellington Place, Wellington Street		RG9/196	23-24
Wellington Street, Rodney Street	1-39	RG9/196	15-23
	Pt 5 & 13	RG9/196	36
West Place, Chapel Street	2-7	RG9/195	50-51
Weston Street, Pentonville Road	1-26	RG9/196	135-141
	1a & 1b	RG9/196	141
Wharton Street, Bagnigge Wells Road	1-35	RG9/192	66-73
Whisken Street, St John Street Road	36-62	RG9/199	77-90
White Conduit Place, White Conduit Street		RG9/195	82-83
White Conduit Street, Chapel Street		RG9/195	83-87
White Lion Buildings, White Lion Street		RG9/195	28-29
White Lion Street, Islington High Street			
	1-pt 45	RG9/195	1-9
	Penitentiary	RG9/195	33-34
	55-105	RG9/195	33-43
(Part 46 and 47-54 MISSING FROM Wilderness Row, Gos			

1861 London street index

London is divided into about 36 registration districts, depending on the particular year (see Appendix 7). After you have found in which registration district your particular street falls by consulting the index to London streets (see 6(i)), go next to the appropriate index in one of the London street index volumes on the shelves holding the finding aids for your particular census year. These follow the series lists on the shelves and include the Western and Northern districts, the Central and Eastern districts, and the Southern districts of London from Kensington to Greenwich. They do not include West Ham which, although considered part of London now, was in Essex in the nineteenth century.

Each street index has a title page showing you the sub-district divisions and giving the piece numbers which cover those sub-districts. The index itself lists

Bram Stoker, Theatrical Manager M.A. (RG 11/77, f. 4, p. 1)

the streets, buildings, terraces and areas together with house numbers. Each entry is followed by two columns of figures. The first is headed 'To Order Your Film' (or 'To Select Your Film' or 'The Piece Number of Your Film') and provides the reference of the film you require. The second column is headed 'To Find Your Place on the Film' and gives you a folio number, or set of folio numbers, where a particular street will appear on the film. All documents are foliated before being filmed as a security measure to ensure that nothing is omitted from the filming and to provide a reference number when you need to refer to a particular page. These numbers are stamped on the top right-hand corner of every other page of the document, the page without a folio number being identified as the reverse of the preceding page and taking the same folio number.

```
                      1871 CENSUS

                     STREET INDEX

                REGISTRATION DISTRICT 12

                     H O L B O R N

Sub-Districts    1   St. George the Martyr    RG10/369-372
                 2   St. Andrew Eastern       RG10/373-375
                 3   Saffron Hill             RG10/376-378
                 4   St. James Clerkenwell    RG10/379-383
                 5   Amwell                   RG10/384-387
                 6   Pentonville              RG10/388-391
                 7   Goswell Street           RG10/392-395
                 8   Old Street               RG10/396-398
                 9   City Road                RG10/399-403
                 10  Whitecross Street        RG10/404-408
                 11  Finsbury                 RG10/409-411
```

Title page to an 1871 street index

THE PIECE NUMBER OF YOUR FILM Folios	TO FIND YOUR PLACE ON THE FILM

Column headings in a street index

Folio number

You may not necessarily find a street all in one place on the film. The enumerator liked to save his shoe leather, and while going up and down a street would also take in side streets where they occurred, before returning to the main street to continue his rounds. You may, therefore, often find more than one sequence of folio numbers beside a street name, and also streets which are continued in other registration districts where boundaries cut across a road. This is explained more fully in 'Finding your place on the film' (pp. 32–43).

In 1841 there is one slight difference in the referencing system. You will need a book number as well as a folio number to identify the whereabouts of your street. The foliation in that year started again at the beginning of each book in

HM Alexandria Victoria, The Queen (HO 107/1478, f. 645, p. 19)

the box, so that if you cite an 1841 reference without its book number but using a folio number only, it could mean one of several folios with the same number but in different books. The book number together with the folio number identifies a specific page. The book number can be found on every frame of the film as part of the filming strip and on the title page of each book (where the foliation begins at 1). There it looks like a fraction, the upper number being the piece number and the lower the number of the book.

1841 book number

Filming strip

4 Country street indexes

The country street indexes are much the same as the indexes to London registration districts. Places with a population of over 40,000 in the nineteenth century were street indexed. For a list of indexes available see Appendixes 8–13.

STREET INDEX TO THE 1861 CENSUS		
CROYDON	TO ORDER YOUR FILM	TO FIND YOUR PLACE ON THE FILM
Street		Folios
Croydon Lodge, St James Road	RG9/450	31
Croydon Road	RG9/451	118–121
Crystal Palace Lodge	RG9/451	142
Crystal Palace Road, Norwood	RG9/450	78–79
Crystal Terrace	RG9/451	7–10
Dagnall Park	RG9/450	166–168
Dale House, Beaulah Hill	RG9/451	42
Dalletts Cottages, Merton Rush	RG9/453	89–90
Daltons Court, Church Street	RG9/449	71–72
Daniels Cottages, Whitehorse Road	RG9/450	48–49
Dartmill Cottage, New Town	RG9/451	12
Deerfield, Beaulah Hill	RG9/451	39

1861 country street index

Charles Landseer, Historical Painter (RG 9/56, f. 124, p. 36)

Most have a separate list of public houses, institutions and shipping at the back and some years have some items grouped together under a heading such as Schools or Caravans (this heading includes any travellers even if they are sleeping in a tent). Individually named buildings, terraces and groups of cottages are included, and each index has a title page showing the name of the registration district and its division into sub-districts. Country street indexes do not, however, show house numbers except for larger towns in 1881.

Hamlets included in any township are mentioned as entries in the index itself and not usually on the title page. Over the years other places with a population of less than 40,000 have acquired a street index, or a partial street index where not all of the registration district has been covered. These are not part of the normal run of PRO indexes but have been included in the bound street indexes for each year on the reference shelves. They are few and only exist for some years from 1841 to 1871. They are listed in Appendix 13.

5 A list of available surname indexes

The PRO does not itself compile surname indexes. There are, however, numerous surname indexes produced by family history societies and published in booklet form, although many are now produced on microfiche and CD-ROM instead. (For the whereabouts of microfiche readers see the plan of the search room in Appendix 6 (p. 83).) Most societies begin with the 1851 census but many have progressed to the other years. They generally regard the PRO at the FRC, Society of Genealogists and the Family History Library at Salt Lake City as places of deposit. The Genealogical Society of Utah and the Federation of Family History Societies indexed jointly the whole of the 1881 census, which is now available at the FRC as one of the family history databases and is available elsewhere on CD-ROM. The PRO has indexed the 1901 census and it is possible to interrogate the database for the surname you seek.

Many of these surname indexes are available in the census room and more are added each week. The lists of what is available are on the shelves in the reference area with each year of the census in colour coded binders. If one is available for the place you want make a note of the registration district number and go to the drawers in area 6 on the plan in Appendix 6 where the surname indexes are housed. The filing drawers contain printed surname indexes, filed by registration district number and in colour-coded envelopes. Some of the indexes are in typewritten format and are in binders in a bookcase in the same area. Many surname indexes are now produced on fiche and the envelope will direct you to the carousels nearby. If there is no envelope for your registration district in the year you wish to search, this means that as yet none has been donated.

John Sanger, 'Equestrian Troupe' Circus Proprietor (RG 9/2943, f. 114, p. 6)

If the surname you want is listed it should also show the reference of the film you need and a folio number which will help you to find your place on the film. See pp. 32–43 for an explanation of how to locate places by the use of folio numbers.

6 Additional finding aids

6(i) Index to London streets

When looking up an address in any of the London censuses it is essential to be sure of its registration district. In some census years there are as many as thirty-six registration districts in central London, and you can waste many hours seeking a street in the wrong district unless you do some homework first. It is not enough to consult a map, for it will not tell you the boundaries of a registration district in relation to the street names, and knowing that a street is in Marylebone today does not necessarily mean that it fell within the boundaries of the Marylebone registration district. It may have been borderline and, in census terms, it may have fallen within Pancras or Hampstead. There is one sure way of finding out.

In 1887 the Metropolitan Board of Works published *Names of Streets and Places within the Metropolitan Area*. This is an instantly forgettable title so the book is referred to as 'London streets and their localities'. It provides a complete list of London streets, terraces, buildings, roads, etc. (except for those which changed their name or were abolished before 1855), with the name of the nearest main road in a central column and the name of the parish in which they lie in the right-hand

Name.	Postal District.	Locality.	Parish.	Year.
Wharves (The)	S.E.	River-side	East Greenwich	
Wharves (The)	W.	Uxbridge-road	Hammersmith	
Wharncliffe-street	E.	Bonner-street	Bethnal-green	1860
Wharton-place	E.	School-house-lane	Ratcliff	
Wharton-road	W.	Sinclair-gardens	Hammersmith	
Wharton-street	E.C.	King's-cross-road	Clerkenwell	
Whateley-road	S.E.	Kent-house-road	Beckenham	
Whateley-road	S.E.	Lordship-lane	Camberwell	
Whatman-road	S.E.	Brockley-road	Lewisham	1887
Wheathill-road	S.E.	Croydon-road	Penge	1887
Wheatley's-cottages	S.E.	Ravensbourne-street	Greenwich	
Wheatsheaf alley	S.W.	Bishop's-road	Fulham	
Wheatsheaf-lane	S.W.	South Lambeth-road	Lambeth	
Wheatsheaf lane	S.W.	Upper Tooting	Streatham	
Wheatsheaf-whf.-alley	E.C.	Upper Thames-street	City	

Index to London streets

John Bird Sumner, Archbishop of Canterbury (HO 107/1571, f. 291, p. 4)

column. The parishes named in the right-hand column are in most cases the same as the names of the appropriate London registration district but occasionally the name of the sub-district. In this case a quick check in the table pasted to the front of the book will explain the whereabouts of a particular place by giving the name and number of the registration district in which it occurs. Then you can proceed confidently to the correct street index volume.

6(ii) Index to abolished London street names

Sometimes London streets cannot be found in street indexes even though a birth, marriage or death certificate of a similar date clearly states the address. This is because street names changed, renumbering took place, or new streets were built. When an enumerator collected his information it was quite possible that people still referred to their address by a recently discontinued name, or that a renumbering of a street obscured the fact that, for example, 86 King's Road was once 2 Victoria Cottages. The cottages may still be there with their name on the brickwork, but each of the individual cottages has acquired a number that is part of the road it is on, in place of the number of its particular position in the

Wet—Whi 550

Name of Street or Place.	Locality.	Postal District.	Parish.	Metropolitan Borough, or City.	County Electoral and Parliamentary Division.	Ordnance sheet 5 ft. to 1 mile.	Reference to Municipal Map.	Name approved.	Alterations. (1856–1928)			
									Date of Order.	No. of Plan.	Names abolished.	Numbers assigned.
Wetherell road	Victoria park road	E.9	Hackney	Hackney	S. Hackney	vii.-29	38-12	1868	30.v.79	2346	Providence row Louisa cottages Albert terrace	1-55 (cons.)
Wexford road	Nightingale lane	S.W.2	Battersea	Battersea	S. Battersea	x.-80 90	17-37	1894				
Weybourns street	Garratt lane to Steerforth st.	S.W.18	Wandsworth Borough	Wandsworth	Cen. Wandsworth	x.-99	13-40	1913				
Weybridge street	Culvert road	S.W.11	Battersea	Battersea	N. Battersea	xi.-31	18-30	1863	13.ii.12	..	Carpenter street	
†Weymouth dwellings	Sayer street	S.E.17	Newington	Southwark	S.E. Southwrk.	vii.-95	23-24					
Weymouth court	Sayer street	S.E.17	Newington	Southwark	S.E. Southwrk.	vii.-95	23-24					
†Weymouth court	Weymouth street	W.1	St. Marylebone	St. Marylebone	St. Marylebone	vii.-52	21-17					
Weymouth mews	Weymouth street	W.1	St. Marylebone	St. Marylebone	St. Marylebone	vii.-52	20-17	..	1.iii.89	4196	.. ..	1-45 (cons)
Weymouth mews	Weymouth terr.	E.2	Shoreditch	Shoreditch	Shoreditch	vii.-37	33-14					
Weymouth street	Gt. Portland st. to High street, Marylebone	W.1	St. Marylebone	St. Marylebone	St. Marylebone	vii.-52	20-17		3.iii.76	1756	Upper Weymouth street	1-71; 2-48
Weymouth terrace	Hackney road	E.2	Shoreditch	Shoreditch	Shoreditch	vii.-27 37	33-13		10.xi.06	508	White's cotts. Prospect terrace Albion place Elizabeth cotts.	1-127 2-142
Whalebone court	Moorgate bldgs.	E.C.2	City of London	City of London	City of London	vii.-66	30-18					
Whalebone passage	Tokenhouse yard	E.C.2	City of London	City of London	City of London	vii.-66	30-18					
Wharf road	Pritchard's road	E.2	Bethnal green	Bethnal green	N.E. Beth. grn.	vii.-28	35-13		9.xi.88	4126	.. ..	1-25; 2-22
Wharf road	Latimer road	W.10	Hammersmith	Hammersmith	N. Hammersmith	vi.-66	7-19		7.xii.83	3209	Eastbourne terr. Wharf terrace	1-43; 2-30
Wharf road	Uxbridge road	W.12	Hammersmith	Hammersmith	N. Hammersmith	vi.-76	8-21					
Wharf road	Ferry street, Cubitt Town	E.14	Poplar Borough	Poplar	S. Poplar	xii.- 2 11 12	44-26					
Wharf road	City road	N.1	Shoreditch and Finsbury	Shoreditch Nos. 1-21 Finsbury Nos. 22-35	Shoreditch 1-21 (cons.) Finsbury 22-35 (cons.)	vii.-35	29-14					
Wharf road	Frogmore	S.W.18	Wandsworth Borough	Wandsworth	Putney	x.-58	12-34	..	21.v.89	4227	Haydon's cotts.	1-43 (cons)
Wharfdale road	Caledonian road	N.1	Islington	Islington	W. Islington	vii.-33 34	25-13		24.vii.68	789	Wharf road Gordon terrace Albert place Albert terrace St.Stephen's la. Haverford terr.	1-69; 2-82
Wharfedale street	Coleherne road	S.W.10	Kensington	Kensington	S. Kensington	x.- 8	12-26					
†Wharncliffe gardens	Grove road, St. John's Wood road and Cunningham pl.	N.W.8	St. Marylebone	St. Marylebone	St. Marylebone	vi.-49 50	15-15					
Wharncliffe street	Hartley street	E.2	Bethnal green	Bethnal green	N.E. Bethnal green	vii.-38 39	37-14	1860	4.xii.85	3585	.. ..	1-11; 2-22
Wharton street	King's Cross road	W.C.1	Finsbury	Finsbury	Finsbury	vii.-34 44	26-15					
Whateley road	Lordship lane	S.E.22	Camberwell	Camberwell	Dulwich	xi.-67	33-35	..	3.xii.86 31.i.05	3797 6047	Whateley terr.	1-55; 2-34 49-85
Whatman road	Brockley rise	S.E.23	Lewisham	Lewisham	W. Lewisham	xi.-89	32-37	(1867)	15.xii.03	..	Whatman street	2-56
‡Wheatlands road	Tooting Bec road	S.W.17	Wandsworth Borough	Wandsworth	Balham and Balham	xv.- 1	18-41	1906	27.x.22	7232		

Index to abolished London street names

Joseph Tussaud, Artist (RG 10/164, f. 13, p. 20)

terrace or group of cottages. Much renumbering of London streets in this way took place in the 1850s and 1860s.

The way round this problem is to look in the four volumes, 'London streets alterations and abolished names (1912)', which rejoice in the full title *London County Council List of Streets and Places Within the Administrative County of London shewing Localities, Postal Districts, Parishes, Metropolitan Boroughs, Electoral Divisions, Ordnance and Municipal Map References Together with the Alterations in Street Nomenclature and Numbering since 1856.* The PRO has the revised edition, compiled by the Superintendent Architect of the Council and published in 1912. You will see in many cases a 'date of order' in a column after the street name; this means that at that date an order went through for some adjustment in the street name. Some time after this date the change would have been put into effect. These volumes, however, like the index to London streets, do not include the names of streets abolished or changed before 1855.

6(iii) Shipping index

Shipping on rivers and within territorial waters was included in the census returns at the end of the districts where the ships lay, but it was not until 1861 that shipping on the high seas and in foreign ports was enumerated, and then only some of it. Returns from such ships are found in the special shipping schedules at the end of the returns from 1861 onwards. There is an index to the names of ships compiled from the 1861 schedules, on the shelves with the 1861 reference books, and also a set of microfiche which indexes all the people on board, for 1861 only. Ask at the enquiries desk.

Name of Ship	Whereabouts	Reference RG 9
BACCHUS	Bristol	4498
BACCHUS	Llanelly	4530
BADGER	North Sea	4450
BALBIC	Liverpool	4507
BALCLUTHA	A.S.	4438
BALFOUR	Dudgeon Light	4463
BALLARRAT	At Sea	4458
BALLARAT	Dieppe	4459
BALLINASLOE	Birkenhead	4502
BALLINDOLLAGH	At Sea	4446

1861 shipping index

James Burn, Editor of the ABC Railway Guide (RG 10/1322, f. 61, p. 12)

6(iv) List of ecclesiastical parishes

It frequently happens that a particular place required by a searcher is an ecclesiastical district and cannot be found in the list of places because the census was enumerated in civil parishes. Obviously the ecclesiastical district exists, but it is necessary to determine in which civil parish it rests. To do this, consult the list of parishes. This is a four-volume book, bound in black, that will tell you in most instances the name of the ecclesiastical parish in the left-hand column followed by the civil parish in the next column. There is also a column giving the poor law union, which is the same as the registration district. Armed with the name of the registration district and appropriate civil parish you can discover the reference by the normal procedure.

Once you have the film on the machine and you have turned to the civil parish indicated, you will see, if the enumerator has done his job correctly, that there is a box at the top of the page labelled 'ecclesiastical district', which contains the place name you originally sought. If it does not, turn back to the title page of that enumeration district where you may find mention of the ecclesiastical district and be reassured that it has been enumerated in that part of the film.

ESSI] 188							
Parish or Place.	United with or included in	'Division.	County.	Description.	Tax Survey.	Poor Law Union.	Collector of I. R.
1 Essington -	Essington, &c. -	Cuttlestone -	Stafford -	Tp.	STAFFORD -	Cannock -	Wolverhampton.
2 Estacott -	(Northoe P.) -	Braunton -	Devon -	Ham.	BARNSTAPLE -	Barnstaple -	Exeter.
3 Eston -		Langbaurgh East	Yorks -	Tp.	STOCKTON -	Middlesbrough -	Sunderland.
4 Estyn -	Caergwrley, &c.	Mold -	Flint -	Ham.	CHESTER -	Hawarden -	Chester.
5 Estynallou -	Bodlith, &c.	Cynlleth and Mochnant.	Denbigh -	Tp.	WREXHAM -	Oswestry Incorporation.	Chester.
6 Etal -	(Ford P.) -	Glendale -	Northumb.	—	ALNWICK -	Glendale -	Newcastle.
7 Etchells -	Northenden, &c.	Stockport -	Cheshire -	L.T.P.	STOCKPORT -	Altrincham and Stockport.	Manchester.
8 Etchells in Northern	Etchells in Northern, &c.	Stockport -	Cheshire -	Par.	STOCKPORT -	-	Stockport.
9 Etchilhampton -	Etchilhampton, &c.	Devizes -	Wilts -	L.T.P.	CHIPPENHAM -	Devizes -	Bath.
10 Etchingham -	-	Hastings Rape (Battle).	Sussex - Yorks	Par.	HASTINGS -	Ticehurst -	Canterbury.
11 Etherolwick Etherley -	(Escomb Tp.) -	Darlington Ward	Durham -	Ham.	DARLINGTON -	Auckland -	Sunderland.
12 Ethy -	St. Winnow Lostwithiel.	-	Cornwall -	—	BODMIN -	-	Plymouth.
13 Ethirick -	(St. Dominick P.)	East Middle -	Cornwall -	Ham.	LAUNCESTON -	Liskeard -	Plymouth.
14 Eton -	-	Stoke -	Bucks -	Par. & L.B.	WINDSOR -	Eton -	Reading.
15 Etton -	-	Peterborough -	Northampton	Par.	PETERBOROUGH	Peterborough -	Lincoln.
16 Etruria -	(Shelton P.) -	Pirehill North -	Stafford -	—	STOKE-ON-TRENT	Stoke-on-Trent -	Derby.
17 Etterby -	Brunstock, &c. -	Eskdale Ward -	Cumberland	L.T.P.	CARLISLE -	Carlisle -	Carlisle.
18 Ettiley Heath -	(Sandbach P.) -	Northwich -	Cheshire -	Ham.	CREWE -	Congleton -	Chester.
19 Ettingshall -	(Bilston P.) -	Seisdon -	Stafford -	Ham.	WOLVERHAMPTON	Wolverhampton -	Wolverhampton.

List of ecclesiastical parishes

The Duchess of Orleans (HO 107/1604, f. 122, p. 37 – f. 123, p. 38)

6(v) List of churches and chapels wherein marriages are solemnised according to the rites of the established church 1871

As its rather lengthy title suggests, this volume is a list of churches and chapels, grouped alphabetically by the name of the registration district into which they fall. Its value is that, having located a family in the census returns, a searcher may need to continue the hunt for families in parish registers. After consulting this book you will know which parish or nonconformist registers to consult. This list is part of an annual series from which the one for 1871 has been selected for use in the census room. Ask at the enquiries desk if you wish to consult it. You may find when seeking parish records in the area in an earlier period that not all the churches listed in 1871 will be in existence. The ecclesiastical census of 1851 (HO 129, held at the PRO, Kew) surveys places of worship at that date.

Do not forget that if ancestors do not seem to appear in appropriate parish registers, they may have been nonconformist. Many researchers disregard non-conformist records, many of which are held in the PRO in the record series RG 4 to RG 8 and made available in the census room at the FRC as well as at Kew, because they assume that the family has always been Anglican. Nonconformity was very popular in the nineteenth century, especially amongst some classes of

List of registered churches and chapels for the solemnisation of marriage

William T Mitford, Magistrate Deputy Lieutenant (RG 11/140, f. 79, pp. 13–14)

people such as industrial workers, artisans and tradesmen, and your ancestors may have become involved in the current trend. The nonconformist registers in the record series RG 4 are indexed on the *International Genealogical Index*, a copy of which is available in the census room (see Shorney, *Sources for the History of Non-Conformity* (PRO Readers' Guide 13).

6(vi) London street directories

The London street (or trade) directories are not only useful for tracing individuals from their known trades or professions, but can also help when you are faced with

Street directory for London

John Ruskin, Author of Works on Architecture and Painting (HO 107/1475, f. 598, p. 16)

multiple entries for a street in a street index. Where there are several references in a street index, and no indication as to which one contains the house number you want, turn to the street directory. Look up your street, find your house number and note the names of the two side streets (written in italics) nearest to your house number, and then go back to the street index. Look up the references to the side streets and select similar references from the selection given for your long street. Remember that some streets may run on into another registration district.

The FRC makes available the street directories for the year following a census year in order to allow for the compilation and printing of information gathered in that census year. Even so, as is often the case today, these may have errors at the time of going to press, and many chose not to be included; so, if persons are not listed in the directory under the address you expect, you may still find them there on the film. The copies of the London directories will be found on the shelves with the rest of the finding aids for the year.

6(vii) Maps

Instinctively one turns to a map when difficulties are encountered in locating a place, either while searching in the indexes or after finding a birthplace on the microfilms. Sometimes it is much quicker to turn to a gazetteer or one of the additional finding aids before going to a map because most maps do not relate to census divisions.

The FRC makes available a book of parish maps, known as the Phillimore Atlas, arranged by county, published by the Institute of Heraldic and Genealogical Studies at Canterbury and available for purchase from them, from the PRO shops and from the Society of Genealogists. This is useful when a parish does not include the family you are looking for and you need to cast your net wider and search the surrounding parishes.

There are also four incomplete sets of maps in the PRO at Kew which give the boundaries of the registration districts, sub-districts and the civil parishes. One set, for 1861, is of large-scale maps covering the London registration districts only. The set for 1871 lacks maps for large towns. The set for 1891 shows registration districts in silhouette so that if the name of a place strays over its boundary it will be found on another map. Note your registration district number when using the 1891 set since that is the way the outline maps are arranged within the counties. A copy in colour of each map is available at the FRC in area 5 on the room plan in Appendix 6. There is also a set of maps for 1921 which is not made available at the FRC.

Dr Charles Mark [Karl Marx], Philosophical Author (HO 107/1510, f. 260, p. 11)

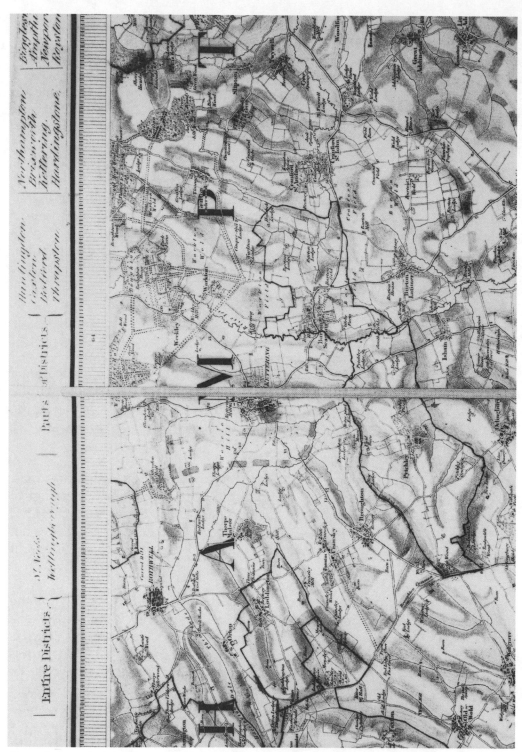

Part of a map showing Kettering and the surrounding census districts (RG 18/52)

These maps are most useful when an individual large house or a tiny hamlet cannot be found in street indexes or other finding aids. Once the place is located on the map the parish containing it can be determined by noting the place name, which has a pink line through it within the thin red boundary line. Then note the sub-district by observing the pink boundaries within which the place falls, and the large pink spot on the place which gives its name to the sub-district. Finally, note the green boundary lines and the green spot on the place which is the name of the registration district, and return to the lists and indexes for the year you wish to research.

The London Metropolitan Archives has published a list of known eighteenth-century maps of London; the Guildhall Library and the Bishopsgate Institute also have useful map collections. An *A–Z of Georgian London* and an *A–Z of Victorian London* have been published by the London Topographical Society; equally valuable is the series of Victorian Ordnance Survey Maps published by Godfrey.

The appropriate local record office or local history or family history societies may be able to help if you are in difficulties with any particular place. They will have local knowledge not available in the census room.

The Society of Genealogists has published a map showing London registration district boundaries in relation to borough boundaries and the boundaries of the local family history societies. This is available at the Society bookshop.

6(viii) Population tables

Once the census returns had been thoroughly checked by the enumerators and their supervisors, the information collected was published as a set of Parliamentary Papers; copies of these for all census years may be seen at the FRC. The tables, like the series lists, are arranged in numerical order of registration district, and give the breakdown of an area into registration districts, sub-districts and townships. They also give the acreage of each township. Then follows a count of houses and population for each place, both for the year being enumerated and for the previous census year. The footnotes give useful additional information: e.g. why a local population varied markedly from the previous census, or where institutions (as defined on p. 38), or lists of railway navvies, may be found. Copies of these tables are kept in the census room in case clarification is required of places falling within a registration district or information is needed about the fluctuation of population in an area. A list of these publications will be found in the Bibliography.

John W Millais, Proprietor of Houses (HO 107/1509, f. 75, p. 14)

610 YORKSHIRE—35. WEST RIDING.—Area ; Houses and Inhabitants, 1851 an		Area in Statute Acres.	HOUSES.				
SUPERINTENDENT REGISTRAR'S DISTRICT.			1851.			186	
SUB-DISTRICT.	Parish, Township, or Place.		Inha-bited.	Un-inha-bited.	Build-ing.	Inha-bited.	Un-inha-bited
	495. TODMORDEN.						
1. HEBDEN BRIDGE	*Halifax, part of* Parish—[a]						
	Wadsworth - - Township	10080	957	166	–	923	156
	Erringden - - Township	2980	333	47	1	371	44
	Heptonstall - [aa] Township	5320	882	127	2	790	170
	Stansfield, *part of* [a] -[aa] Township [viz., the Lower Third Division.]		353	95	3	320	98
2. TODMORDEN -	*Halifax, part of* Parish—[a]	} 5920					
	Stansfield, *part of* [a] - Township [viz., the Middle Third and Upper Third Division.]		1132	102	11	1351	6
	Langfield - - Township	2620	752	41	55	890	3
	Rochdale, part of Parish—[b]						
	TODMORDEN and Walsden } Townp. (*Lancashire*) - - }	–	1481	114	31	1790	6
	496. SADDLEWORTH.						
1. DELPH [ba] - -	Saddleworth, *part of* † - Township } (*part of Rochdale* Parish.[b]) }	} 18280	1819	230	10	2048	16
2. UPPER MILL [bb] -	Saddleworth, *part of* (W)† Township } (*part of Rochdale* Parish.[b]) }		1548	105	18	1770	11
	497. HUDDERSFIELD.						
1. SLAITHWAITE -	*Huddersfield, part of* Parish—[c]						
	Slaithwaite - - Township	2320	553	29	7	575	1
	Marsden { in *Huddersfield* Parish [c] -	2050	103	9	6	138	1
	Tnp.‡ [d] { in *Almondbury* Parish §[e] -	5061	407	50	4	428	2
	Almondbury, part of Parish—§[e]						
	Lingards - - Township	500	159	4	–	149	
	Linthwaite, *part of* ‖ -[f] Township	809	264	13	–	309	1
2. MELTHAM -	*Almondbury, part of* Parish—§[e]						
	South Crosland - Township	1560	536	36	2	582	3
	Meltham - - Township	4525	684	42	20	795	7
3. HONLEY -	*Almondbury, part of* Parish—§[e]						
	Honley (W) - -[g] Township	2790	1077	35	17	987	18
	Netherthong - - Township	850	228	13	5	223	3

Population tables

6(ix) Miscellaneous topographical indexes

As indexing of census returns has progressed over the years much useful information has been collected to assist in identifying the whereabouts of places and particular addresses, especially in London.

> 1. County variations and divided parishes
> 2. Parishes and localities
> 3. Divided streets
> 4. Renumbered streets
> 5. Missing streets

Item 1 above is an index which may help to identify places which do not occur in the series lists where you would expect to find them. It is located on the shelves in the reference area.

The other four indexes, which may be useful when searching for places in London, are available at the enquiries desk. Identifying a particular part of London can be quite complex as some streets appear in more than one index. Ask a member of staff to help you if you need to use these volumes.

Henry Ryman, Manager – Stationery (RG 11/195, f. 4, p. 1)

From reference to microfilm

Once you have discovered your reference, take a black 'dummy' box from the shelves near the enquiry desks and go to the area containing the microfilm readers and film cabinets (see p. 83 for a plan of the FRC). The films are in numerical sequence of reference number and you will see that the cabinet drawers are clearly labelled with the first and last references held within them. When you open the drawer, you will find there is a locking mechanism which allows only one drawer in a stack to be opened at any one time. The reference numbers are marked on the side of the film boxes; select the one you need and replace it with the black box, but make a mental note of its number. Then go and find your seat number which corresponds to the number on your black 'dummy' box. The seats are numbered by a label on the top of each machine. When you return the film, retrieve the black box. Please be sure to put your film back in the right drawer when you have finished with it. The boxes are colour coded to match the reference books for each year. It is easy to put the film in the right sequence numerically but in the wrong drawer for the year. When you have finished with your seat replace the black box on the shelf that you got it from.

Microfilm readers

To thread your reel of film onto the microfilm reader, attach the reel to the spindle on the left-hand side of the machine. Next thread the film from the bottom of the reel to the right, under the gate and onto the empty spool on the right-hand spindle. Do not thread the film over the top of the right-hand reel but carry on moving the film to the right under the empty spool and bring it up on the outside of the spool and over the top in an anti-clockwise direction. Put the end into the slot in the centre of the spool, as shown in the diagram on p. 32. When going through the film quickly in order to reach a particular piece number, open the gate of the microfilm reader; there is then less wear and tear on the film. Once you are in the right piece number, close the gate and start looking at the detail.

You will find two or three lens settings directly above the gate which are changed by turning the bevelled wheel to the right or left as required. The on/off switch is to the right of the machine, and the focus button is in the front of the base. Microfilm readers must be switched off when not in use to avoid over-heating and damage to the film, which is liable to happen within even a few minutes.

Alfred Tennyson, Poet Laureate (HO 107/1698, f. 493, p. 26)

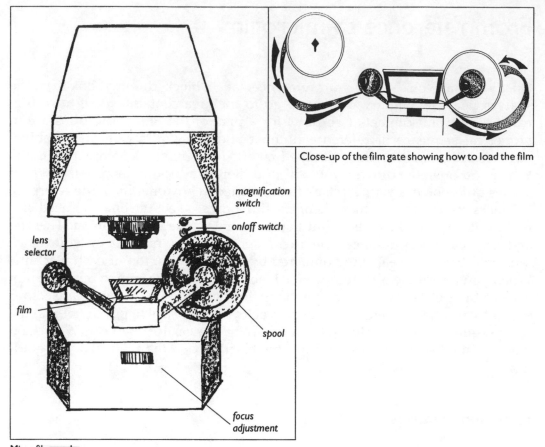

Close-up of the film gate showing how to load the film

magnification
switch

on/off switch

lens
selector

film

spool

focus
adjustment

Microfilm reader

If the plastic spool is worn in the middle so that it will not run smoothly when turning the handle, ask a member of staff at the copy service desk to change it for you.

Finding your place on the film

Once you have the film correctly threaded onto the machine you can start your search. Without having seen the original enumerators' books it must be difficult to understand the system you find. Remember that the enumerators handed out schedules to householders in the week preceding census night and collected them on the Monday morning immediately after the Sunday night – it was always a Sunday – of the census (see Appendix 1 for the dates of the 1841–1901 censuses). The enumerator then had to enter the information from these schedules into a book and provide a description of his district on the title page.

Edwin Landseer, Artist (HO 107/678, book 4, f. 8, p. 9)

Some went further and provided maps or comments about the people they met. Most listed either the streets included in their enumeration district or the streets *surrounding* their area (in other words, streets which do not appear in the following enumeration district but which define the area to be covered because they surround it). In 1891 the style of these title pages was altered to help clarify the parts of administrative divisions occurring in each enumeration district (see p. 64). Even then it is difficult to discover exactly where some smaller places occur, as the enumerators, having completed these new title pages, did not always repeat the place names in the box headings at the top of each page (see also p. 72). The enumerator also had to complete a summary page of the totals of males and females and buildings he had encountered (see p. 35).

Each of these books, therefore, has a title page, a page of instructions and a printed example of a completed form, a page of tables for the enumerator to complete, an abstract of totals and a page declaring that the information is correct (see pp. 34–7). It is only after all this that the information about individuals begins.

The enumerators' books are bound into folders, about five or six at a time depending on their size. When these folders were filmed, they were first foliated for security, as a check that all had been included on the microfilm and to provide a precise reference when needing to identify a page. This means that the top right-hand corner of every

Folio number

other page is stamped with a sequence of numbers that begins and ends within that one folder, except in 1841 and 1851 when each box of folders was foliated throughout. Consequently, when you obtain a reference for 1841 or 1851, it will cover more than a similar reference for other census years. You will find that your piece number (the third element of your reference, see Appendix 4) may cover more than one film, whereas for 1861–1901 you may get several piece numbers to a single film or fiche. So when you put your film onto the machine, depending on which year you are looking at, you need to make sure that you are in the right part of the film.

Each frame on the film has a strip down one side, or along the bottom, with the reference number on it. Since you will be selecting either a film with several different references, or a film that is only part of one reference, you need to check these strips until you have found the right reference for your place. Once you are into that part of the film you can narrow your search further.

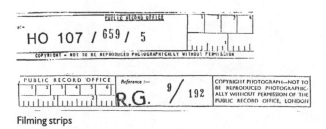

Filming strips

William Hamley, Toy Dealer (RG 9 / 170, f. 30, p. 17)

58

Superintendent Registrar's District *Clerkenwell*

Registrar's Sub-District *Amwell*

Enumeration District, No. 4

Name of Enumerator, Mr. *Henry Dyer*

DESCRIPTION OF ENUMERATION DISTRICT.

[This description is to be written in by the Enumerator from the Copy supplied to him by the Registrar. Any explanatory notes or observations calculated to make the description clearer or more complete, may be added by the Enumerator].

"From and excluding Lower Great Percy Street, both sides along east side of Bagnigge Wells Road, including Police Court and Police Station along Kings Terrace North taking Wharton Street both sides — Comprising —

Nos 31ᴬ to 25ᴬ and 32 to 39 Lower Great Percy Street Nos 27 and 28 Bagnigge Wells Road Police Court and Police Station Nos 1 to 8 Kings Terrace North and Nos 1 to 53 Wharton Street and Percy Grove

1861 title page to an enumerator's book (RG 9 / 192, f. 58, p. i)

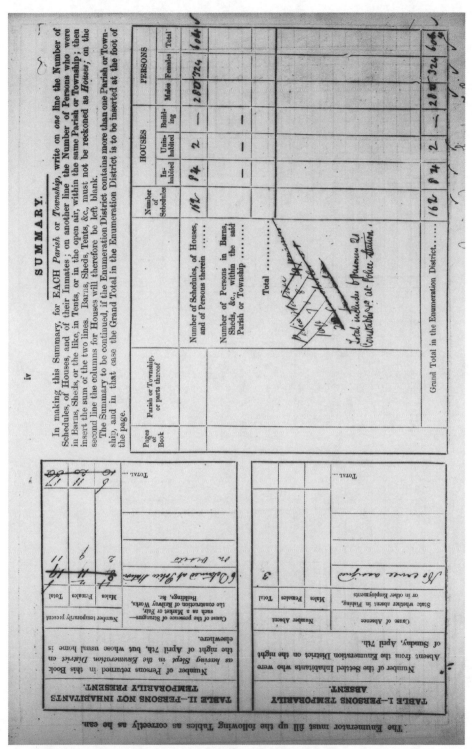

Summary page of an enumerator's book (RG 9 / 192, f. 59, p. iv)

ABSTRACT OF TOTALS IN THE FOLLOWING PAGES.

Page	No. of Schedules	Houses Inhabited	Uninhabited	Building	Males	Females	Total
1	5	3			12	11	23
2	6	3			12	12	23
3	9	4			14	10	24
4	7	4			9	15	24
5	4	2			10	12	22
6	6	4			8	15	24
7	7	4			22	1	23
8	5	2			14	10	24
9	6	3		1	10	13	23
10	8	2			10	14	24
11	7	4			9	15	24
12	4	2			8	15	23
13	6	3			10	12	22
14	6	3			11	13	24
	80	40	1		159	167	326
15	5	3			10	16	26
16	5	4			12	13	25
17	8	3			9	14	23
18	7	3			11	12	23
19	6	3			13	10	23
20	6	3		1	9	12	21
21	10	3			12	12	24
22	8	5			12	13	25
23	6	4			8	16	24
24	7	6			7	16	23
25	8	5			13	11	24
26	6	3			5	12	17
27							
28							
	82	44	1		120	157	277
29							
30							
31							
32							
33							
34							

NOTE.—The number of Persons in Barns, Sheds, Tents, &c., must be entered against the page in which they occur, and the words "*Barns, Sheds,* &c.," as the case may be, must be written in the spaces for Houses.

RECAPITULATION.

Pages	No. of Schedules	Houses Inhabited	Uninhabited	Building	Males	Females	Total
1 to 14	80	39	1		159	164	326
15 to 26	82	44	1		120	157	277
29 to 34							
TOTAL ...	162	84	2		279	324	603

Abstract of totals from an enumerator's book (RG 9 / 192, f. 60, p. v)

vi

I SOLEMNLY declare that the Account of the Population and Houses of the District for which I am Enumerator, contained in this Book, has been truly and faithfully taken by me, and that, to the best of my knowledge and belief, the same is correct.

Witness my hand this *Fifteenth* day of April, 1861,

Henry Ayer **Enumerator.**

I CERTIFY that I have carefully examined the Account of the Population and Houses contained in this Book, and have satisfied myself by comparing it with the Householders' Schedules or otherwise, that the instructions have been punctually fulfilled and all defects supplied and inaccuracies corrected so as to make it as accurate as possible.

Witness my hand this *29th* day of *April* 1861,

W. Saunders **Registrar.**

I CERTIFY that I have examined the Account of the Population contained in this Book, and that the Registrar has duly performed the duties required of him in regard to the same, and that no inaccuracies have been discovered therein which have not been duly corrected, as far as has been possible.

Witness my hand this *13th* day of *April May* 1861,

Wm. Robert Hartin **Superintendent Registrar.**

Statement of accuracy from an enumerator's book (RG 9 / 192, f. 60, p. vi)

Superintendent Registrar's District *Clerkenwell*   Enumeration District, No. *4*

Registrar's Sub-District *Amwell.*   Name of Enumerator, Mr. *Henry Dyer*

DESCRIPTION OF ENUMERATION DISTRICT.

[This description is to be written in by the Enumerator from the Copy supplied to him by the Registrar. Any explanatory notes or observations calculated to make the description clearer or more complete, may be added by the Enumerator].

From and including Lower Great Percy street, both sides, along east side of Bagnigge Wells Road, including Police Court.

1861 title page to an enumerator's book

Page 20]

Parish [or Township] of
St James Clerkenwell

Road, Street, &c.,

Parish box heading and page number

If you picked up a reference from the series list, then you need to start looking at the title pages of the books, which occur at regular intervals – remember there are five or six of these in each piece number – or at the boxed headings on each page for your place. Bearing in mind that each civil parish can contain numerous hamlets, tithings or townships, you need to search for your particular one before applying yourself to the information on the page.

If you have found your reference from a street index for 1841–1901 or a surname index, you will be seeking a particular folio number. Remember that each folio number covers two pages, so do not just look at the page on which the folio number is stamped but also on the unstamped following page which is its reverse (see p. 45). Some older street indexes which may still be found in some reading rooms away from the FRC and PRO, Kew, refer to an enumeration district rather than a folio number, which is written by the enum-erator on the top right-hand corner of the title pages of the books on the film.

101

Folio number

Enumeration District, No. 4

Enumeration district number

There are two exceptions to the above. Institutions such as workhouses, hospitals, asylums or military barracks, providing they contained at least two hundred inhabitants, were given the status of enumeration districts in their own right, and are found at the end of each district on special forms which have no address column (see pp. 39 and 40). The information given is sometimes not very useful as birthplaces are frequently not known ('N.K.'), but other records covering these particular categories may yield the information required. Similarly, shipping – both in territorial waters and on inland waterways – was recorded on special shipping schedules and these too are found at the end of the districts (see p. 23). For an example of a completed shipping schedule see pp. 41 and 42. Un-fortunately not many of these shipping schedules survive in the 1891 returns.

Laurence S. Lowry, aged 3 (RG 12/3157, f. 108)

38

Superintendent Registrar's District _Stockton_

Registrar's Sub-District _Sedgefield_

ENUMERATION BOOK

FOR

* _The Durham County_

Lunatic Asylum

* Here insert the Name and Description of the Public Institution.

The above-mentioned Institution is situate within the Boundaries of the

† Parish [or Township] of	City or Municipal Borough of	Municipal Ward of	Parliamentary Borough of	Town [not being a City or Borough] of	Hamlet, or Tything, &c., of	Ecclesiastical District of
Sedgefield						

† Draw the pen through such of the words as are inappropriate.

Title page to an institutional return (RG 9 / 3696, f. 38)

Completed page showing institutional entries (RG 9/3696, f. 43)

CENSUS OF THE POPULATION, 1871

SCHEDULE FOR VESSELS.

PREPARED UNDER THE DIRECTION OF ONE OF HER MAJESTY'S PRINCIPAL SECRETARIES OF STATE, PURSUANT TO THE ACT OF 33 & 34 VICT., c. 107.

NAME of VESSEL	*Peace*
Official Number (if any)	65,200
PORT or Place to which she belongs	*Hull*
Her Tonnage	70
Her DESCRIPTION, and the Trade in which she is employed	Smack — Fishing Trade
NAME of MASTER	*Henry Bennett*

Place at which the Schedule is delivered to the Master and the Date of Delivery.

Position of the Vessel at Midnight, April 2nd, 1871.

To the MASTER or PERSON in CHARGE of the VESSEL.

1. You are requested to insert the particulars specified on the other side respecting all the persons who slept or abode on board the Vessel **ON THE NIGHT OF APRIL 2nd**, in compliance with an Act which passed the House of Commons and the House of Lords in the last Session of Parliament, and received the assent of Her Majesty The Queen on the 10th of August, 1870.

2. This Paper must be properly filled up **ON THE MORNING OF APRIL 3rd**, signed by yourself and delivered to the appointed Officer, who will apply to you for it.

[3. Should you be the **MASTER** of a **BRITISH VESSEL** and be out *on the night of April 2nd*, on a Coasting or short foreign voyage, you must fill up the Form on April 3rd, and deliver it with the *LEAST POSSIBLE DELAY either at the Custom House of the British Port of arrival, or to the Officer who may apply for it.*]

4. Persons who refuse to give correct information incur a penalty of Five Pounds.

5. The Return is required to enable the Secretary of State to complete the **EIGHTH** Census, which is to show the exact numbers, ages, and professions of the people—their arrangement in different ranks, professions, and trades—their distribution over sea and land—their increase and progress during the last ten years

Approved,

H. A. BRUCE,

Home Office, Whitehall, Dec. 9th, 1870.

GEORGE GRAHAM,
Registrar General.

NUMBER of PERSONS belonging to the Vessel **ON SHORE** on the night of Sunday, **APRIL 2nd:—**

	ABSENT ON SHORE. [Names not entered in the Schedule on the other side.]		
	Males	Females	Total
Crew			
Passengers			
		Total	

EXAMPLE of the MODE of FILLING UP the SCHEDULE.

	Name and Surname	Condition	Age of Males	Age of Females	Rank or Occupation	Where Born	If (1) Deaf-and-Dumb (2) Blind (3) Imbecile or Idiot (4) Lunatic
1	Alexander Fawcett	Married	42	...	Master	Durham, Sunderland	—
2	John Johnson	Married	34	...	Mate	Lanarkshire, Glasgow	—
3	George Saunders	Unmarried	25	...	A. B. Seaman	Yorkshire, Hull	—
4	Thomas Smith	Unmarried	21	...	O. Seaman	Middlesex, London	—
	[Here will follow all the Names of the Crew, Passengers, Visitors, and others].						
	Mary Fawcett	Married		36	Master's Wife	Yorkshire, Whitby	—

Shipping schedule for the fishing smack 'Peace' from Hull (RG 10/4797, f. 134)

131

Peace

LIST of OFFICERS, CREW, and OTHERS on BOARD of the SHIP or VESSEL named the _____ on the NIGHT of SUNDAY, APRIL 2nd, 1871.

	NAME and SURNAME (With, after the Name of the Master, the Names of the Officers and Crew, and then the Names of Passengers and of all other Persons.)	CONDITION (Write "Married" or "Unmarried," "Widower" or "Widow," against the Names of all Persons except Young Children.)	AGE [Last Birthday] of Males	Females	RANK or OCCUPATION (State here the rank of the Officers, and the rating of the Men and Boys of the Crew. The rank or occupation of Passengers and of all other Persons should be stated as fully and clearly as possible.)	WHERE BORN (Opposite the Names of those born in England, write the County and Town, or Parish. If born in Scotland, Ireland, the British Colonies, or the East Indies, state the Country or Colony. If born in Foreign parts, write the particular State or Country, and if also a British Subject, add "British Subject," or "Naturalized British Subject," as the case may be.)	If (1) Deaf-and-Dumb (2) Blind (3) Imbecile or Idiot (4) Lunatic (Write the respective Infirmities against the name of the afflicted Person; and if so from Birth, add "from Birth.")
1	Henry Bennett	Married	37		Captain	Ramsgate Kent	
2	Henry Scott	Unmarried			Mate	London Middlesex	
3	William Scott				Fisherman	London Middlesex	
4	John Richard Smillet				Fisherman	London Middlesex	
5	Henry Smillet		15		Boy	Hull Yorkshire	
6							
7							
8							
9							
10							
11							
12							
13							
14							
15							

I declare the foregoing to be a true Return, according to the best of my knowledge and belief.

Witness my Hand. (Signature) _Henry Bennett_

Completed schedule for 'Peace' (RG 10/4797, f. 134)

Remember, therefore, that films for different years vary in their content. The following paragraphs explain each year's characteristics, and will also apply to finding the right frame on a microfiche when censuses are produced in that form.

1841 Each film covers a series of small books. Each book has its own identifying number, marked on the first page. For example, piece HO 107/659 has books 659/1, 659/2 and so on. Each book has its own folio numbers on the top right-hand corner of every other page and may contain more than one enumeration district, the numbers of which are to be found on the title page of each district. This book number is also included on the identification slip which appears on the side or bottom of each frame of the film.

1841 book number

1851 Each piece has folio numbers which run right through the piece no matter how many separate books and enumeration districts are covered: they appear at the top right-hand corner of every other page. If a piece consists of more than one reel, the folio numbers covered by each reel are shown on the boxes. Wind on the film until you reach the folio numbers you were given in the reference books.

Folio number

1861–1891 Each film covers a series of piece numbers which are foliated separately. Wind the film on to your piece number and look there for your place. If you have used a street index you can find your place by the folio numbers in the top

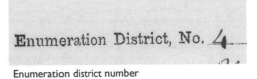

Enumeration district number

right-hand corner of every other page, but some older indexes don't give you folio numbers, just an enumeration district number, so turn to the enumerator's title page at the start of each district and look for your enumeration district number in the top right-hand corner. Then wind the film on and look for your street in that enumeration district.

Always make a careful note of reference numbers; you may need to refer to the same piece again in the future, and the numbers are proof that the facts you state are true and can be checked by the sceptics.

Charles Kean, Tragedian (HO 107/734, book 6, f. 7, p. 5)

Title page of book 5 for 1841, St James, Clerkenwell (HO 107/659, book 5, f. 1)

To return to your place on the film

As you may need to refer to the entry again, you should note down the exact reference while the film is on the reader. You will need the reference number that you used to select the film, the folio number and the page number. You will also find this referencing system essential to enable you to pass on specific information about your research to other census users.

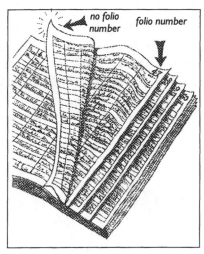

Foliation

Before the original returns were microfilmed, folio numbers were stamped on the top right-hand corner of every other page. The rule is that a page without a folio number is the reverse of the preceding page and therefore has the same folio number when quoted for reference. To refer to a specific page of a folio you only need to give the folio number and state whether it is the recto (first side or right side) or the verso (reverse side) of the folio. Many people, however, prefer to use page numbers to identify which side of the folio they are referring to. If you use this method beware of the many sequences of page numbering used in the census. The page numbers are printed on each page and are preceded by the word 'page' except for 1841 and 1851 when they appear in the centre and at the top of each page.

If your search is in the 1841 census you will also need a book number, because each piece covers a series of small books which have their identifying number marked on the first page and are foliated separately. It can be found on the reference strip on the side or on the bottom of the frame.

1841 book number

Having found what you want, make a note of the folio and page numbers and then roll back the film to the first folio of that sequence, where you will find folio '1', and look at the bottom of that page, which will have a figure like a fraction with the piece number above and the book number below. The book number is also noted on the reference strip on the side or the bottom of each frame of the film. Check that you have correctly recorded these two numbers.

Filming strip

William Gladstone, MP (HO 107/739, book 3, f. 8, p. 8)

Photocopies

If you would like a photocopy of part of the census returns, before removing the film or fiche from the reader you need to identify the frame you require (note that poor quality original documents or scratched films will not reproduce high quality copies). If you are unsure how to identify the correct frame, *leave the film or fiche on your reader, switch the reader off, and consult a member of staff.*

To obtain photocopies you need to know the full reference number including:

1841: the book number and the folio number, e.g:

HO 107/659,   book 5, folio 3

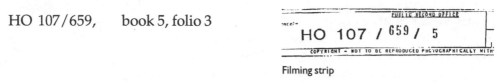

Filming strip

1851–1901: the folio number and the page number, e.g:

HO 107/1595	folio 243 page 29
RG 9/1053	folio 136 page 1
RG 10/653	folio 122 page 6
RG 11/1253	folio 43 page 12
RG 12/456	folio 29 page 16
RG 13/2245	folio 36 page 5

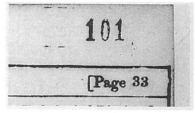

Folio number and page number

See also Appendix 4.

Any postal applications for photocopies must have full correct references including folio numbers and page numbers. Please note that the FRC does not offer a postal copy service and any such request would need to be forwarded to the PRO at Kew addressed to the Record Copying section.

There is one other factor you should consider if you plan to reproduce a document (i.e. to quote substantial parts of it or to print photographs or other copies of it). All census returns are subject to Crown Copyright (see Appendix 3).

Please note that surname indexes other than the 1881 surname index and the *IGI* cannot be photocopied. They are the copyright of the family history societies who compiled them and application should be made to the appropriate society.

To obtain a copy from film or fiche you can make a copy yourself or if you are at the FRC, ask a member of staff to produce the copy, which will cost a little more.

George Du Maurier, Artist 'Punch' (RG 11/166, f. 99, p. 19)

In order to pay for the self-service copies you will either need to purchase a copy card from the copy desk or pay by cash. Once the card has been used you can recharge it by putting coins in the slot adjacent to the copy machines which are located at various points round the edge of the reading room.

- Purchase card from copy desk

- To recharge your card either:

  Insert card, press green button, insert coins

  or

  Take card to copy desk (cash, cheque, credit card)

- To remove card press green button

Using a microfiche reader

If you are using the 1901 fiche at Kew or in many other record offices, when using a microfiche reader you need to collect the card on the front of each reader and put it in place of the fiche you have selected. To insert the fiche into the reader, pull the plate on which it sits towards you and the glass cover will rise, enabling you to place the fiche under it. Insert the fiche with the fiche header on the edge nearest to you. Push back the plate unit and the image will appear on the screen. The plate slides to and fro and up and down to enable you to move from frame to frame. If the image is unclear adjust the focus knobs. There is also a black lever which enables you to change the magnification if you prefer. When you put the fiche away, don't forget to replace the card on the reader for the next person.

Edward Howard, Cardinal Archbishop of Frascate, Lunatic (RG 12/807, f. 13)

Microform reader/printers

Machines to make copies
from fiche are
labelled 'fiche
only'

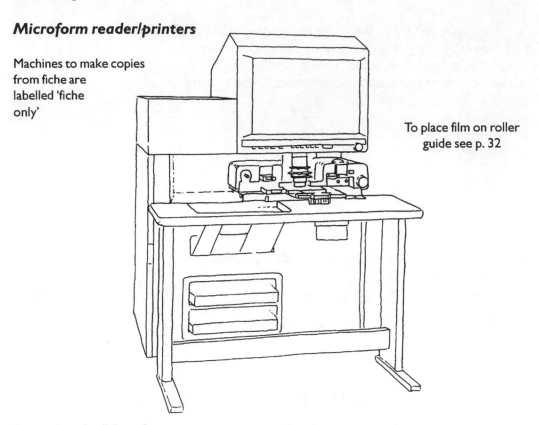

To place film on roller
guide see p. 32

Instructions for fiche only

1. Pull fiche carriage towards you, place fiche between the two pieces of glass and push the carriage back in place.
2. If the image is back to front take out the fiche, turn it over, and replace it between the pieces of glass.
3. If the image is upside down or off at an angle use the rotation knob to straighten it up the right way.
4. Select either A4 or A3.
5. Move the carriage so that the frames you wish to copy appear on the screen. If A3 is selected, the whole screen will be copied. If A4 is selected only the middle section of the screen will be copied.
6. Use the zoom lens to enlarge or reduce the image.
7. Focus the image.
8. Place either a copycard or cash into the Cashkard machine located to the side of the copier (please note that no change can be given).
9. Press green print button to make a copy.
10. If your print is cutting off part of the image, reduce the magnification (blue wheel).

To print

1. Insert Cashkard or money into the Cashkard machine to the right of this copier.
2. Select paper size (A3 or A4). The boundary for A3 is indicated by the black rectangular line bordering the screen. The boundary for A4 is the sub-divisions within the black rectangle. Select the central area.
3. Set exposure of print by using lighter/darker buttons. Make sure the green auto light is on
4. Use zoom control (blue ring) to set the desired size of image within A3/A4 parameters as described in step (2). If the image is still too big or too small, seek assistance.
5. Adjust focus if necessary (grey ring).
6. Press green print button.

If you would rather a member of staff printed your copies for you, please take your film and references to the copy desk. The charge is 35p per sheet. A maximum of 25 prints can be done at any one time. This service is subject to availability of staff.

Alfred Tate, Retired Sugar Refiner (RG 121/548, ff. 21–22)

Accessing censuses by computer

For the 1881 and 1901 censuses you do not need to use the finding aids mentioned above although they exist if you require them. This is because these two years have been indexed in another way which enables you to find your way around the censuses by using your computer to find it for you.

1881 census

For 1881 the 26 million entries were all transcribed and indexed by the Federation of Family History Societies. Access can be achieved by looking at the collection of family history databases at the FRC reading room on networked computers. There are three indexes generated by the database which includes all the transcribed material. One allows you to search the census by surname within a county, by surnames of people born in the same parish or by surnames within a place being enumerated. What you get is the full transcript of the entry you select with all the information viewed on the same page of the returns. The number of the LDS film or the PRO reference number is also on each frame so that you can then check the original returns on microfiche or microfilm to verify the surnames and other information.

1901 census online

For 1901 a further improvement is available. Not only have all the 32 million entries been transcribed in order to provide an index available on the internet which you can search right across the whole of England and Wales, but also the original returns have been digitised, which means you can view an image on a computer screen directly from the index. You will have to pay for access to the image but not to the index. If you plan to use the internet access at the FRC you will need first of all to obtain a timed ticket from the 1901 census ticket desk as you do for the fiche and online access at the PRO, Kew.

The way you begin is to key in the web address **www.census.pro.gov.uk** to get to the right part of the internet for your search. This will give you the census home page with a menu bar giving all the options for getting the best out of the service. You can search by *person* or *place*, or you can look for a *vessel* or an *institution*.

To search for a *person* you must enter their last name (if it is double-barrelled you need to search each element separately). If you cannot find them, try

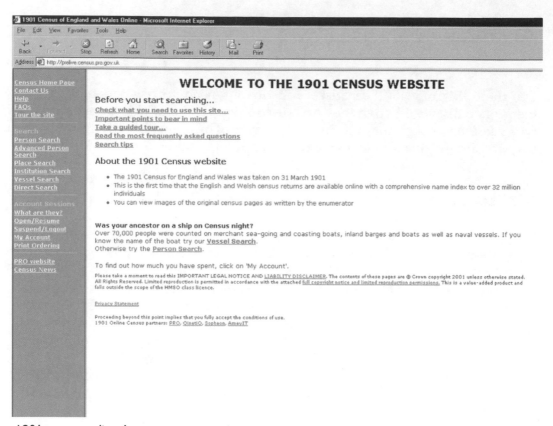

1901 census online: home page

reversing the surname and the first name, as where it is not possible to determine which way round the enumerator has written them, they have been left as they were written in the returns. Where a first name is obviously so but has been entered under the surname it has been put in the right place, i.e. in the first name box. You have to remember, though, that the person supplying the information to the enumerator may have given a nickname or familiar name rather than their full formal first name. So if you can't find them amongst the selection of people given, try using a short name such as Jack rather than John, or Fanny rather than Frances. The good news is that the system will recognise usual abbreviations for first names such as Wm. for William. The other factor which may make it difficult to find someone is if they had a title. The title has been put in the first name box, which means you will get a different entry than expected. As with other searches you have the option, when unsure of the spelling, to put in a wild card in the form of an asterisk (*) for multiple letters or the underscore symbol (_) for just one letter.

Thomas R Joyce, Editor Daily Graphic (RG 12 / 626, f. 28)

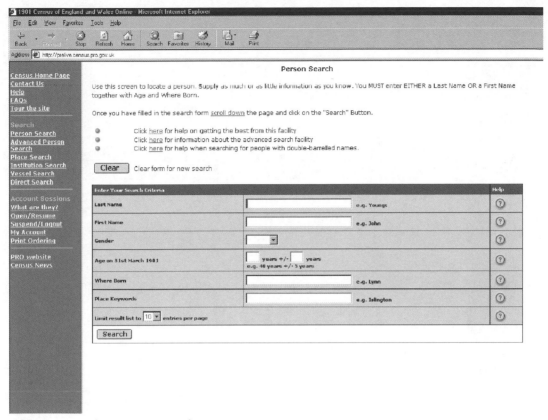

1901 census online: person search screen

There is also an *advanced person search* which allows you to add more information to the simple surname and forename in order to define your selection more precisely. You can add a middle name, gender, birthplace or occupation, to cut down on the number of entries listed in the selection offered.

You can also vary the way a surname is spelt in case either the handwriting or enumerator has confused what was entered into the enumeration books.

To search for a *place* you type in the place name and you will be given a list of all the enumeration books which cover it. You can select the title page of the book and browse onwards or skip to the first page which contains personal information.

Once you have found the person or place you want in the index, you have the option of viewing an image of the original return or viewing a transcription of a

James Lyle, Sugar Manager (RG 12 / 1316, f. 107)

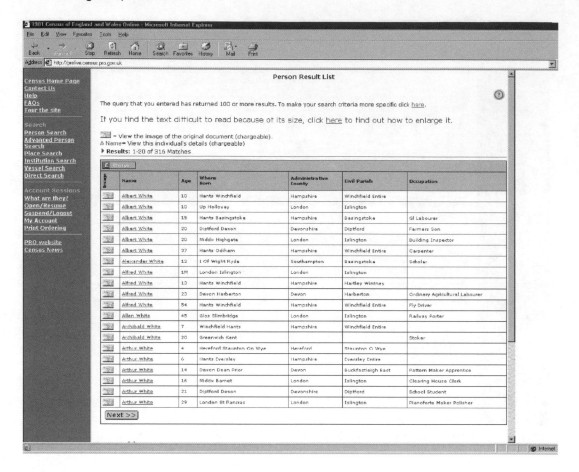

1901 census online: person result list

person's details. At this point you will have to pay to access further information. For a more detailed explanation of how to search the census online, obtain a copy of the PRO's guide, *Census Online: 1901 Census Online User Guide*. It will tell you what capacity your computer needs to access the census and explain the payment options and how to download an image. This information is also available on the website.

A few words about the rules applied to the transcription may help with the understanding of why things may not be straightforward when you search. The transcription, like that for the 1881 census, was done from the original documents and did not aim to correct anything found there – just to record what could be seen and not what was thought should be there. Therefore, if an enumerator made a copying error as he completed his enumeration books after bringing home all the schedules, his spelling is faithfully recorded rather than

John Church, Shoe Manufacturer (RG 12 / 1196, f. 102)

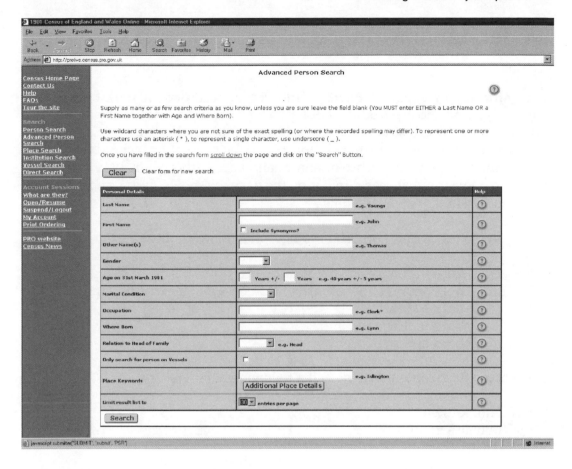

1901 census online: advanced person search screen

the word you might expect to find. After all, you are trying to identify what the returns actually show on the pages.

As with any transcription, handwriting can cause problems. The mis-interpretation of handwriting generally occurs when one letter is mistaken for another, as in the following examples:

a for *o*   *l* for *s*   *e* for *s*   *nn* for *m*   *ll* for *tt*
m for *w*   *w* for *vi*   *k* for *h*

capital *R* for *P* or *K*
capital *J* for *I* or *T* or *F*

v, w, m, n, and *u*
f, g, p, y or *z* in lower case

Charles Harrod, Grocer, Tea Dealer (HO 107/716, book 14, f. 27)

Understanding the returns

The information supplied for each individual recorded in the 1841 census returns is name and age (rounded down to the nearest five years for people over fifteen, though this instruction was not always followed), occupation, and some indication of the area of birth. Relationship to the head of household may often be assumed from the sequence of names and ages, although in 1841 this is not recorded. Divisions between families on the page are shown thus / and divisions between dwellings are shown thus //.

The letters in the 'where born' column have the following meanings:

Y – yes = born in county of current residence
N – no = not born in county of current residence, but born in England or Wales
I = born in Ireland
S = born in Scotland
F = born abroad

The 'occupation' column may have the following abbreviations:

NK – not known
FS – female servant
MS – male servant

The returns for 1851, 1861, 1871, 1881, 1891 and 1901 are more informative. In addition to the information supplied in the 1841 returns, they give the exact ages of the persons enumerated, their marital status, relationship to the head of the household and exact place of birth. The column on the extreme right is the disability column which records whether the individual is 'deaf and dumb', 'blind', and from 1871, an 'imbecile', 'idiot' or 'lunatic'. This final column was not completed as frequently as it should have been (see Higgs, *Making Sense of the Census*, p. 75). In one instance an enumerator has used the expression 'idiot' for the person's occupation (RG 9/2139, f. 64, p. 23). From 1891, returns from Welsh registration districts, and those for Monmouthshire, recorded whether a person was Welsh or English speaking or could speak both languages. More information was added each time a census was taken. For a sample of completed census pages for the years 1841 to 1901 see pp. 55, 57, 59, 61, 63–65 and 67. The returns for 29 Wharton Street show the mobility of the Victorian population.

Benjamin Disraeli, Privy Councillor (RG 9/43, f. 65, p. 12)

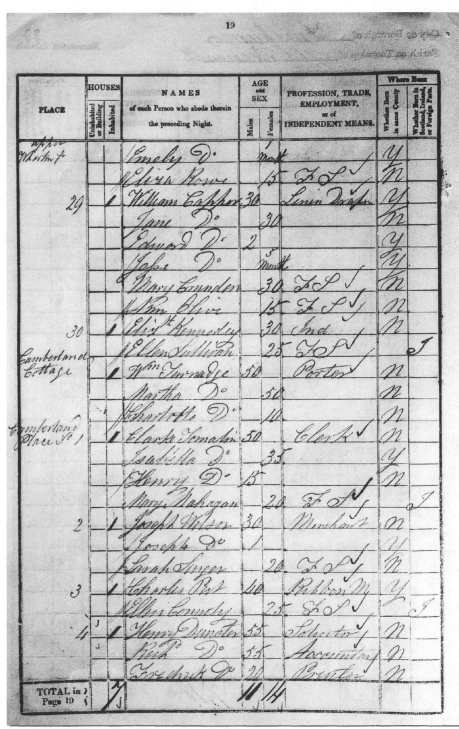

1841 census: 29 Wharton Street is inhabited by William Capper, Linen Draper, and family (HO 107/659, book 5, f. 40, p. 19)

Although the instructions issued to enumerators were very precise there are many instances where enumerators chose to stray from the rules and made observations or used unconventional terms to complete their returns. Title pages were intended to describe the district the enumerator had to cover but were also used by enumerators to add some comments of their own.

An enumerator in Beverley had carefully written out his instruction 'Enumerator must be careful and not take into the account any of the houses in St Nicholas Parish' and added 'Bow-Wow' (HO 107 / 2359, f. 485). Others chose to voice their opinion on the neighbourhood they had been assigned: 'the houses marked thus x x x x in Close Alley are of a bad character consequently the information is doubtful the attention of the authorities has been directed towards them and several are closed' (RG 9 / 2455, f. 67); and one lists the streets he covers with such remarks as 'all highly respectable, occupied chiefly by humble tradesmen, respectable shopkeepers' and so on (RG 9 / 5, f. 90). One was so enthused with his district that he added 'I suppose a more laborious industrious and worthy community is not to be found within any other Enumerator's District' (RG 9 / 432, f. 168). Another made the excuse 'this District being chiefly composed of the lower order of Irish such as Lodging House Keepers, Pedlers, Rag Collectors, Chip Sellers, Bone Collectors, Hawkers of small wares, Beggers, etc. etc. I found it difficult to get at the proper description of some of the parties' (RG 9 / 2291, f. 44). One concluded his summary with the poem:

So here you have the people all
From Brook Lane Farm to Puddingpoke Hall;
And here, in these mysterious pages,
You'll find the girls 'mysterious ages'.
The Sheep, the Wolves, in each vocation,
The Parson, Clerk & Congregation,
The Deaf, Dumb, Blind, the Wise, the Fools,
The Maids, Jades, Wives & Sunday Schools:
Publicans, Tailors, young Beginners,
Farmers & different sorts of Sinners.
Carpenters, wheelwrights & some Sawyers,
But free from Surgeons & from Lawyers!
Long life to all! and may the blushing maids
Next Census swell by splicing Brockford Blades!

(HO 107/1795, f. 49, p. iii)

Nell Gwynne, Orange Seller (RG 11/381, f. 40, p. 13)

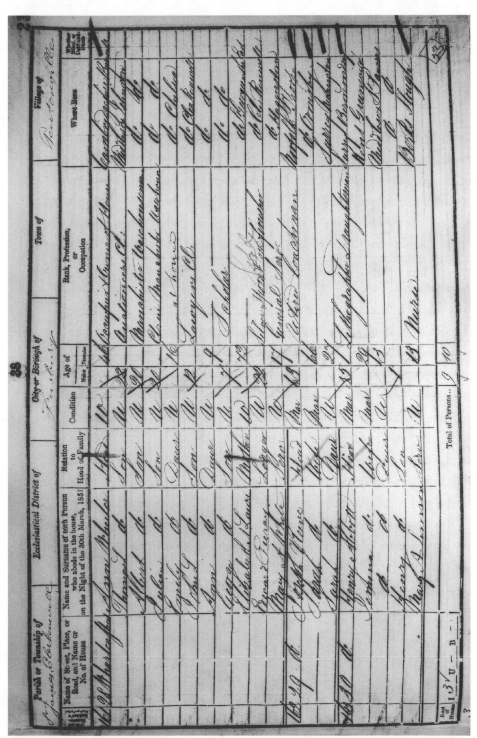

1851 census: 29 Wharton Street is inhabited by Joseph Reeve, a retired coachman, and family (HO 107/1517, f. 23, p. 38)

Other comments made by enumerators relate mainly to the difficulties of gathering the information, but in one case the enumerator felt he had made a mistake in entering the information of a Merchant Navy establishment into his book: 'please see further on for Officers of the Institution which I see should have been entered first. I am sorry that I have been so stupid' (RG 10 / 3775, f. 95, p. 5). The problems of gathering information were expressed by an enumerator in Brightside: 'to ensure accuracy in my district I after delivering the Schedules visited nearly every house a second time. In addition to this on the 1st of April I sent the Bellman through the district to request the Household to fill up their schedules and to supply anyone who might have been omitted during my visit. He says he could not find an omission' (RG 10 / 4693, f. 55). Another difficulty encountered was by an enumerator who said 'the omission of the place of birth in the case of the Lunatics are too frequent; but I was utterly at a loss to make them out from their incoherency' (RG 9 / 647, f. 87, p. 39). In spite of efforts made to provide correct information, the census officer queried the total of houses enumerated in relation to those mentioned by the enumerator; there should have been 400 inhabited houses but the enumerator had only accounted for 288. The local supervisor, when challenged, replied: 'Having seen the Enumerator, Mr Thomas Lilley, he stated to me that the Memorandum Book is correct, as he did it himself, but employed a Junior Clerk to fill up the Enumerator Book which will have Caused discrepencies. Now I may say that Mr Lilley had this same District last time, and I thought he would have done it the best of any, I am very much grieved he has not' (RG 9 / 3841, f. 86). In RG 10 / 4899, f. 66 of Yarm, Stockton, the enumerator, William Thompson, has calculated that he walked 25 miles in the course of 'Distributing the sheddles [sic]' and collecting them up again.

Helen Beatrice Potter, aged 14 (RG 11 / 46, ff. 9–10)

Page 20]

The undermentioned Houses are situate within the Boundaries of the

Parish [or Township] of	City or Municipal Borough of	Municipal Ward of	Parliamentary Borough of	Town of	Hamlet or Tything, &c., of	Ecclesiastical District of

Road, Street, &c., and No. or Name of House	HOUSES		Name and Surname of each Person	Relation to Head of Family	Condition	Age of		Rank, Profession, or Occupation	Where Born	Whether Blind, or Deaf-and-Dumb
	In-habited	Unin-habited (U.), or Building (B.)				Males	Females			

Total of Houses... Total of Males and Females...

Eng.—Sheet D.

1861 census: 29 Wharton Street is uninhabited (RG 9 / 192, f. 70, p. 20)

Missing information: An enumerator in Manchester has explained the lack of information for one particular address by 'gross carelessness on the part of the Lodging Housekeeper. When I informed him to read the Schedule and told him of the penalty, it was all to no purpose, he said he asked their names and they would not tell him' (RG 10 / 4051, f. 160, p. 51). In another case an enumerator has explained 'consequent upon a general Row when tables were turned over, three forms were destroyed and the names of thirty-seven persons, all males, of ages varying from 19 to 60, were lost' (RG 11 / 322, f. 35, p. 16).

There is a note by a Superintendent Registrar: 'the foregoing sheets were filled up by the Reverend W J Palmer, the rector of Mixbury, but being incorect and Isaac Bayliss the Enumerator not being qualified for the Duty; W Thomas Hawkins of Brackley was apointed in his stead' (HO 107 / 886, book 12, f. 13, p. 21). Finally, there is evidence that one person was fined for refusing to give information: 'John Travers will not give any information respecting the persons who abode in his house on the night of June 6th only that the number was 125'. There is a note by the registrar that 'Mr Travers [was] fined £5 at the Mansion House by Sir Peter Lawrie June 23rd 1841' (HO 107 / 732, book 12, f. 6, p. 6).

Harry W Chubb, Lock and Safe Maker (RG 12 / 632, f. 139)

1871 census: 29 Wharton Street is inhabited by John Logan Grover, a solicitor, and his grandson. His housekeeper is not only a servant but is also the mother of his daughter-in-law! (RG10/384, f. 81, p. 56)

Doubts are often expressed that not everyone was included in the census and the remarks of one enumerator above prove this point. Efforts were made, however, to include even those people who had no address such as the three 'unknown men' recorded as 'heated by Japan stoves' in Aston in 1871 (RG 10/3138, f. 106, p. 37) and George Johnson of Barton-upon-Irwell 'living in an empty coke oven' (RG 9/ 2859, f. 74, p. 17). George Jones of Hereford, although usually living in Catherine Street, was recorded as a labourer 'in search of work walking all night'.

One condition, though normally married, unmarried, or widowed, was 'widow bewitched' (RG 10/4407, f. 89, p. 30). Also listed were a changeling (RG 10/4563, f. 82, p. 13) and an orphan 'stolen when a child by gypsies' (RG 9/432, f. 12, p. 18).

Addresses were not always a precise house number and street name. You can find a gin palace (HO 107/1495, f. 565, p. 56), someone living in a shed whose relationship to the head of the family is simply 'friendly' (RG 9/1783, f. 35, p. 22) and 'a factory for beds uninhabited at night' (HO 107/1500, f. 389, p. 48).

The clerks who analysed the information had instructions on how to categorise the many occupations but some recorded must have caused them to scratch their heads as no categories had been provided for them. Amongst the usual means of employment are listed a 'professional wizard' (RG 10/4684, f. 30, p. 6), two fugitive slaves (HO 107/2321, f. 530, p. 27), just 'aristocratic' with the comment in another hand 'Oh Dear' (HO 107/2171, f. 224, p. 19), a squatter from Queensland (RG 11/ 140, f. 28, p. 49), a nymph of the pavé (HO 107/1508, f. 578, p. 36), a runaway slave (RG 9/4127, f. 83, p. 14) and those that defied even those unorthodox descriptions, 'nondescript' (RG 10/1299, f. 21, p. 14) and 'generally useful' (HO 107/ 1528, f. 229, p. 11).

John J Sainsbury, Provision Merchant (RG 12/1061, f. 105)

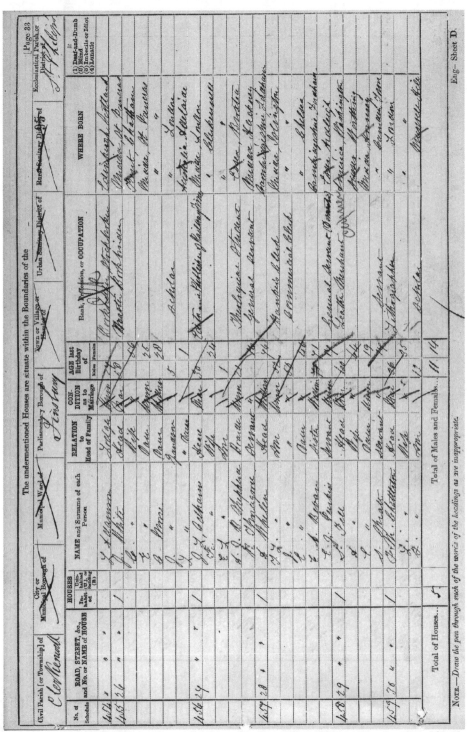

1881 census: 29 Wharton Street is now inhabited by S Fell, Leather Merchant, and family, John Logan Grover being deceased (RG 11/349, f. 95, p. 33)

Title page of an 1891 return for Tunbridge Wells showing the signature of a female enumerator. The following enumeration district was enumerated by her brother and they themselves are enumerated on f. 24 (RG 12/676, f. 2, p. i)

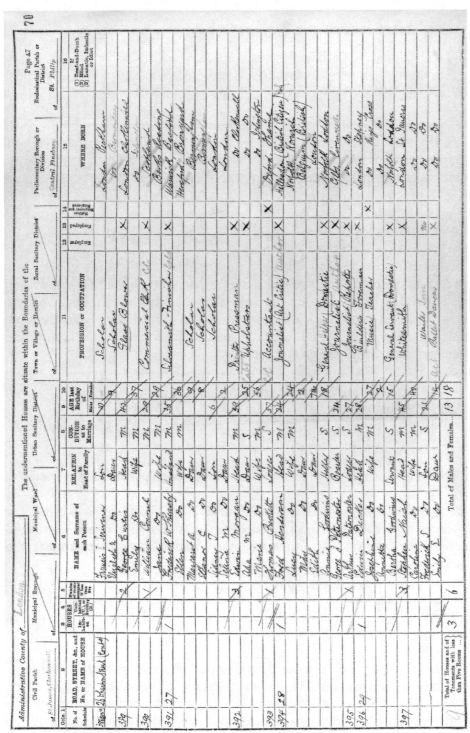

1891 census: 29 Wharton Street has now been divided into two households
(RG 12/224, f. 70, p. 47)

Problems and how to solve them

Misplacing your notebook

It is a good idea to put your name and address in the front of your notebook. Nothing is more soul-destroying than to leave it behind knowing that you will not be revisiting for a few weeks. The staff at a record office will automatically return notebooks that have an address inside the cover.

Failure to record references

Another good practice that may not become apparent until you are well into your research is to *keep an exact reference* of every search you have done, even if it is unsuccessful. It will save hours of duplicate searching when a year or two later you are planning what to look at next and need to remember exactly what you have already examined. It will also be invaluable to relations researching other branches of your family. (See Appendix 4.)

Missing information

Families

If families do not appear where expected there are various possible explanations.

There was some deliberate evasion of the enumerators. Turner, the painter, for instance, is reputed to have spent census night on a boat on the Thames to avoid being enumerated. Evasion was, however, more usually practised among the lowest ranks of society and especially by criminals.

Working-class families appear to have moved from house to house with surprising frequency, and the address taken from a birth or marriage certificate may be out-of-date a few months later.

Many more people leased their houses than do now. This meant that they moved frequently when leases ran out. However, they most probably needed to be within easy walking distance of the same job. If you cannot find a family at a particular address, look round the neighbourhood; they may not be far away.

Henry Irving, Comedian (RG 11 / 95, f. 31, p. 19)

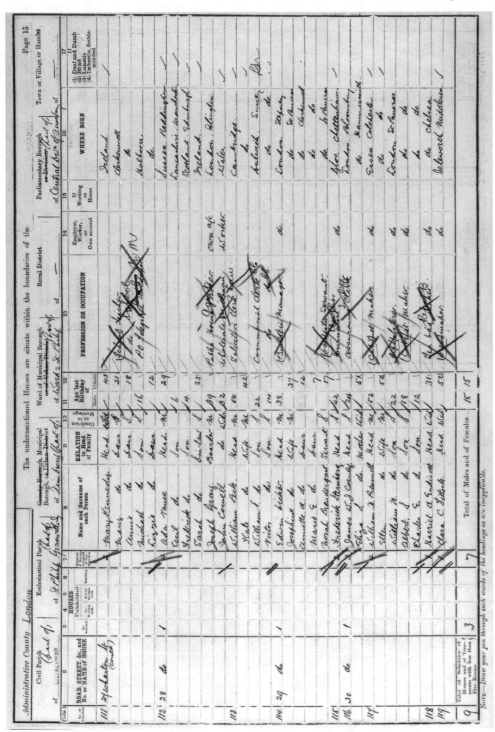

1901 census: Edwin Dickes is still at 29 Wharton Street with another daughter, but the other part of the building has a new tenant (RG 13/252, f. 213, p. 15)

Charles Dickens is to be found staying with Robert Davey, a medical practitioner, at 34 Kepple Street, St George, Bloomsbury. He is listed as 'a visitor aged 39 author born Portsmouth, Hants' and with him, also visitors, are 'Alfred Samuel Dickens married 29 an engineer born Chatham, Kent and Augustus Newsham Dickens married 23 a merchants clerk born London'.

HO 107/1507, f. 206, p. 16

His family, but not his wife, are to be found at their home 1 Devonshire Terrace in Marylebone. Mary Dickens aged 12 is described in the column headed 'Relationship to Head of Household' as daughter of Charles Dickens and her occupation is again 'Daughter of Charles Dickens'. With her are listed Catherine, 11, Francis, 7, Alfred, 5, Sidney Smith, 4, Henry, 2, and Dora Ann, 8 months, with a cook, wetnurse, and nurse.

HO 107/1488, f. 207, p. 9

Mrs Dickens is away from home and can be found staying in a Lodging House with her sister at Knotsford Lodge, Great Malvern, whilst, presumably, taking the waters. The entry reads: 'Catherine Dickens lodger married 35 born Edinburgh and her sister Georgina Hogarth lodger unmarried 24 born Edinburgh'.

HO 107/2043, f. 98, p. 21

The people you are looking for might not have been at home on census night, in which case they will appear at the address where they were staying. In the 1851 census the Dickens family are a very good example of this.

Films

1. Folio numbers may be missing from the sequence: this means that the folio was missed when filming. In this case ask a member of staff if it is possible to see the original or, where this is not possible, to have the original checked at Kew for you.

Henry Trollope, Clerk 2nd class G.P.O. Service (RG 11/266, f. 34)

2. If page numbers are missing from the sequence (but the foliation is correct) the folio did not survive. This situation most often occurs at the back or front of a book which has lost its covers. Unfortunately there is no solution. Another census year should be tried.

3. Some places are missing from the films: these are described as 'MISSING' in the series lists. There is no solution as the enumerators' books disappeared before the returns were transferred to the PRO.

Items missing from indexes

Streets missing from the indexes suggest a number of possibilities:

- the street had not yet been built
- the street was being built at the time
- the street was not yet named as such and the houses are identified by the name of villas, terraces, etc.
- the street was missed by the indexers
- or the folio did not survive and so could not have been indexed

If this happens in a London index look in the index to abolished London street names (see 6(ii) p. 22) to find the date of approval of the street name or the name of the villas, terraces, etc. from which the street was formed. If this does not provide a satisfactory answer then try the street index for another year, and determine at least the sub-district into which it falls; otherwise find another street with the same reference as the street you seek. Then look up the same sub-district or other street in the year you are researching and check the film in case the individual houses or actual street appear in that part of the film and have been missed or disguised in the index.

Items missing from microfilms

1. Houses may be missing from streets: many streets were not numbered until long after they were built and were composed of named villas, terraces, cottages, buildings or individual houses which later remained under those names but were also numbered as part of the longer 'mother street'. Such houses may feature in the index under their former names.

2. Numbers are often missing from streets, since the numerical sequence of houses was erratic in the last century; on the other hand some streets had as many as four separate sequences of house numbers. At a later date this may

William H Lever, Soap Manufacturer (RG 12 / 2871, f. 99)

have been rationalised, but it sometimes pays to continue looking through all references to a street in case the people you seek are indeed living at the house number you expect, but not at the particular house you are looking at because that has a duplicate number. In other words, there might be another 5 Hallam Street further on in the enumeration district. However, not all enumerators bothered to record house numbers and just entered the name of the road.

3. If house numbers are apparently missing from their sequence, this is because house numbers do not necessarily appear in sequence. The enumerator probably took the shortest route through his district. He may have begun at one end of a street (not necessarily number 1), walked down to the next crossroads,

turned into a side street, then continued with the first street, ending up finally with number 1 when he reached the end of his rounds several crossroads later, on the other side of the street in which he started.

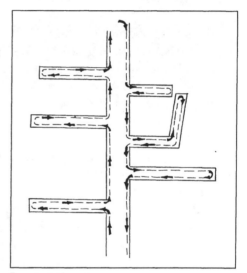

Enumerator's route

If only even, or only odd, numbers are recorded it probably indicates that the street was incomplete and only one side was built. It can also mean, however, that one side of the street was in one enumeration district and the other side of the street was in the next enumeration district, or even that the street was split between several enumeration districts where the boundaries of an enumeration district occur at crossroads. The street index will cross-refer you to other parts of the census where the rest of the street occurs.

In large towns, especially in the Midlands, you will find named buildings and courts listed in the street index. This is where an alleyway leading off a street opens into a courtyard round the sides of which are numerous dwellings, probably several storeys high.

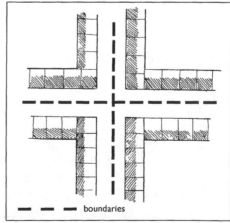

– – – boundaries

Enumeration district boundaries

Francis Reckitt, Manufacturer of Starches, Blues, Black Lead,
and of Machine and Fancy Biscuits by Steam (RG 9/3592, f. 75, p. 35)

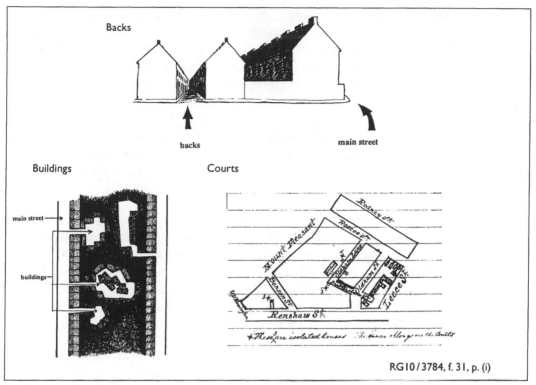

Backs

backs

main street

Buildings

Courts

main street →

buildings →

RG10/3784, f. 31, p. (i)

Back houses, buildings and courts

SUBJECT OF ENQUIRY IN OLDHAM REGISTRATION DISTRICT

Enumeration District 16

From Mr William Ascroft to Mr James L Page, enumerator

Please give a description of the premises designated 'Cellar Dwellings' in the Memorandum Book of this District –

Whether they are Cellars <u>under Houses</u> or separate and distinct habitations called '<u>Cellar Dwellings</u>' -

Please return the Memorandum Book (5 September 1861)

Answer

In answer to your inquiry the term Cellar Dwellings applies to Dwellings under houses in cases where the Ground floor of the Houses are level with the front Street and the Floor of Cellars under the Ground floors are level with a Back Street. The Houses (so called) and the Cellar Dwellings (so called) being in the occupation of seperate tenants – I may somewhat elucidate the matter by saying that the Front Streets have been raised, after the original construction of the Streets and the erection of the Houses: <u>to avoid great declivities</u> and Render the ascent to various parts of the Town easier whilst the Section of the Surface of the Land at the Back has been left in its original State – Afterwards advantage has been taken of making seperate dwellings to face front and back. <u>No connexion existing between such seperate dwellings</u>.

RG 9/3010, f. 51

George Shillibeer, Coachmaker and Undertaker (HO 107/1523, f. 170, p. 22)

HOUSES	
Inhabited	Uninhabited
1	
	2U
1	

House columns

4. If families are missing from houses, they may have been away from home on census night. The purpose of the census survey was to record not only individuals but also buildings, and thus the building in which they normally lived would have been recorded as 'uninhabited'.

If a house was uninhabited on census night it will still be enumerated but will probably be identifiable only by its place between two others. There is a column for uninhabited houses on the enumerator's form.

Missing places: Places missing from a series list means that a particular part of the census did not survive; another year should be tried. Places may be missing from a place-name index because the place being sought may be the name of an ecclesiastical parish instead of the civil parish on which the census was based. The list of ecclesiastical parishes should provide the answer (see 6(iv) p. 24). It lists most place names and in the second column on the page it will tell you in which civil parish they occur. Smaller places than a civil parish can be difficult to locate in the 1891 census. The newly designed title pages enabled the enumerator to break down his allotted patch into various administrative divisions, parts of which would be in his enumeration district and parts in other enumeration districts. Most can be ignored when searching the returns, as the civil parish is the most useful unit for identifying a place in census terms. However, it is very often a township, village or hamlet within this civil parish that one needs to identify. At first glance this breakdown of places on the title page makes this identification easier. However, when you turn to the pages which follow, the box headings are frequently, but luckily not always, ignored by the enumerator which means that location of a particular hamlet or township is impossible unless you happen to know the names of the streets in that hamlet.

Birthplaces: As far as the place of birth entry is concerned, you should remember that many people did not know where they were born, and some others lied about it, fearing that the information might be used to send them back to their home parish, as the Poor Law directed.

Some enumerators, being local men, would not know the place names of the part of the country from where the person they interviewed came. This, combined with a 'foreign' local accent, might produce a place-name spelling that will not occur in any gazetteer or map. If this happens try pronouncing the name given as a local might have done. Perhaps the 'H' has been missed at the beginning.

Ages: Ages in the returns are not always reliable; some people did not know exactly when they were born and there were many reasons for lying about one's age.

John Skeaping, Artist, Portraits in Crayon (RG 12/2913, f. 103)

How to index the returns

At first sight there is a bewildering variety of census indexes; but they fall into clearly defined categories as already noted (see 'Using the reference area' (pp. 13–30)). If you are using the census reading room at the FRC, look in the place-name index for your particular census year, or go to a street index if this is more appropriate. Copies of these indexes are provided by the PRO and are available at Kew for the 1901 census only when viewing that census on fiche.

However, family history societies have for the past two decades been busy compiling another type of index. Different researchers need different pieces of information, and family historians need names before they need places. Total transcripts are never really necessary unless the document is unavailable because it is fragile; researchers should always check an original source rather than rely on someone else's translation or interpretation, which can – even with the best intentions – go astray. It is far more sensible, therefore, to compile an index only. The recommended minimum content for a census index is surname, forename, age, birthplace and reference. If some uniformity had been applied to census indexing it would have been possible to combine local indexes into a national one. The PRO at the FRC has several surname indexes that have been most generously donated by family history societies, and more would be appreciated. In future more censuses will be indexed, as is the 1901 census, and made available on the internet.

Anyone planning to index census returns for publication should adopt the method of referencing used by the PRO. Then, anyone quoting a reference for obtaining a photocopy, or asking for help in deciphering entries, will be talking the same 'language'. Searchers are often asked by the census room staff at the FRC to return to their local record office or library and look again at the film to find the reference required since the information supplied is insufficient to locate the precise entry elsewhere. All this is time-wasting. Individual methods of indexing, while appropriate in the smaller context of a local record office or library, are inadequate when applied to the holdings of the PRO, and it is vital that the complete PRO reference, including the folio and page number, is quoted, though you may find it easier to use the archival terms recto and verso instead of a page number (see also p. 45 for folio numbers and p. 46 for examples of complete references). All the original enumerators' books are foliated before being microfilmed, which means that one can go straight to the page required, but frequently the folio numbers are disregarded by indexers (see p. 45).

Byron Family, Baron Byron BA (RG 11/95, f. 29, p. 15)

Another important factor to consider when planning a census project is the area covered by the index. The census has its own in-built natural divisions for ease of enumeration. It is sensible, therefore, to use these divisions when defining the size of the index. The easiest unit to use, from a searcher's point of view, is that of the registration district. If this is too large to manage then an index to a sub-district is a suitable alternative. Both of these units will be more than one piece number (the archival term for an individual item and the third element of your reference number) and some people do index one piece number only. This can be confusing to a user of the index because it is not easy to define just one piece as being part of a whole. Worse still, some indexers choose a parish as a unit for indexing. Not only does this sometimes mean that you need to index part of a piece number, but also many searchers are unaware of the fact that census parishes are civil ones and 'parish' in its usual form refers to an ecclesiastical district. The question arises, 'which type of parish is being indexed?' When providing an index, therefore, to a particular set of documents, it is much more user-friendly to remain within the natural framework of the documents themselves.

With the advent of the census accessible by computer, the need for stand-alone indexes recedes. The 1901 census is accessed online by means of a database which you can interrogate by name, place, institution or vessel. The 1881 census was indexed by means of a database created when the British Genealogical Record Users' Committee made it the subject of an international project in the 1980s and 1990s. Consequently, the indexing to these two censuses has already been achieved and the conventional process of providing simple census indexes or complete transcriptions in index form is no longer necessary.

For the other five censuses, however, we still benefit from considerable indexing projects carried on by family history societies. Three counties – Devonshire, Norfolk and Warwickshire – have been indexed in the same format as the 1881 census on CD-ROM and microfiche for 1851 only. In future the PRO will be providing access to these earlier censuses for 1841–1871 and 1891 online, and the accompanying facilities as provided for the 1901 census will gradually become available for all census years. Gone will be the tedium of wading through index after index looking for an individual, and a search right across the whole of England and Wales will be possible as it is now for 1901 and 1881. This sort of exercise does not happen overnight but gradually we will be able to access all census material by using a computer to find something for us, be it a place, an address or a person. We will then be able to discard the small indexes which take so long to search. However, a lot of work has to be done first to make this possible and meanwhile we will use all the finding aids now available to search the earlier censuses wherever we view them and in whatever form.

Gilbert K Chesterton, Pupil, St Paul's School, London (RG 12/895, f. 122)

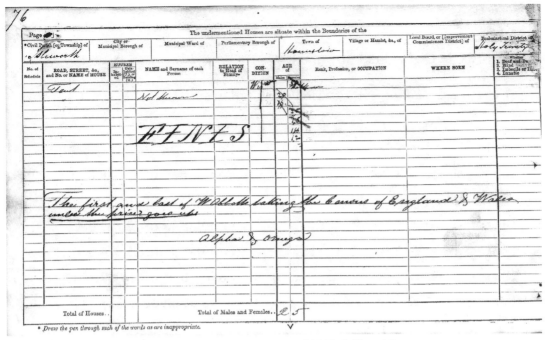

Not all enumerators were happy in their work! (RG 10 / 1313, f. 43, p. 44)

Rudyard Kipling, Author (RG 12/896, ff. 76–77)

Appendixes

Appendix 1: Dates and population

The dates for the taking of the census are as follows:

		Easter	
1841	June 6	April 11	Population of 15,914,000
1851	March 30	April 20	Population of 17,928,000
1861	April 7	March 31	Population of 20,066,000
1871	April 2	April 19	Population of 22,723,000
1881	April 3	April 17	Population of 25,974,000
1891	April 5	March 29	Population of 28,999,725
1901	March 31	April 7	Population of 32,527,843

Rowland Hill, Secretary to Post Master General (HO 107/1492, f. 52, p. 7)

Appendix 2: Census divisions

1 London within LCC boundaries; see map on p. 78

2 South Eastern – Surrey and Kent (extra-metropolitan), Sussex, Hampshire, Berkshire

3 South Midland – Middlesex (extra-metropolitan), Hertfordshire, Buckinghamshire, Oxfordshire, Northamptonshire, Huntingdonshire, Bedfordshire, Cambridgeshire

4 Eastern – Essex, Suffolk, Norfolk

5 South Western – Wiltshire, Dorset, Devon, Cornwall and Somerset

6 West Midland – Gloucestershire, Herefordshire, Shropshire, Staffordshire, Worcestershire, Warwickshire

7 North Midland – Leicestershire, Rutland, Lincolnshire, Nottinghamshire, Derbyshire

8 North Western – Cheshire, Lancashire

9 Yorkshire

10 Northern – County Durham, Northumberland, Cumberland, Westmorland

11 Welsh – Monmouthshire and Wales

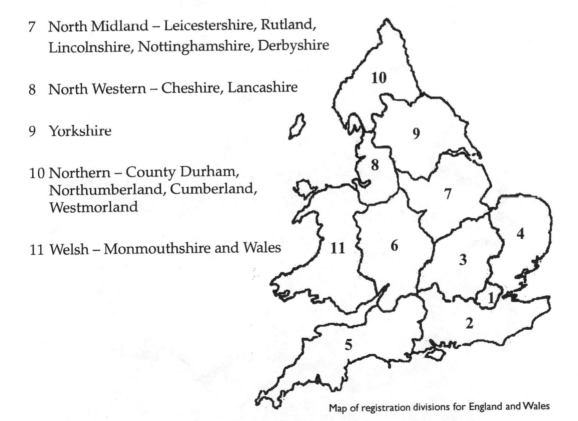

Map of registration divisions for England and Wales

Sir Francis Palgrave, Knight, Deputy Keeper of Public Records (HO 107/1492, f. 53, p. 8)

Division 1

1	Kensington	19	London City
2	Chelsea	20	Shoreditch
3	St George Hanover Square	21	Bethnal Green
4	Westminster	22	Whitechapel
5	St Martin in the Fields	23	St George in the East
6	St James Westminster	24	Stepney
7	Marylebone	25	Poplar
8	Hampstead	26	St Saviour Southwark
9	Pancras	27	St Olave Southwark
10	Islington	28	Bermondsey
11	Hackney	29	St George Southwark
12	St Giles	30	Newington
13	Strand	31	Lambeth
14	Holborn	32	Wandsworth
15	Clerkenwell	33	Camberwell
16	St Luke	34	Rotherhithe
17	East London	35	Greenwich
18	West London	36	Lewisham

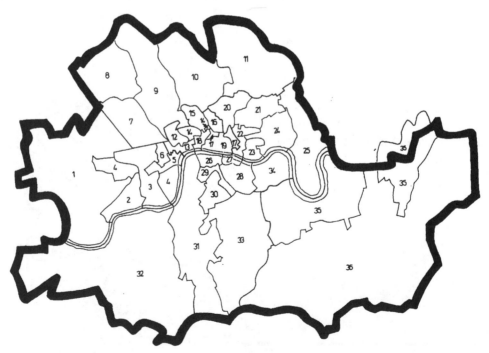

Map of London registration districts

Charles Dickens, Gentleman (HO 107/680, book 14, f. 12, p. 18)

Appendix 3: Copyright in census returns

All British census returns are Crown Copyright. Unauthorised reproduction of the returns – whether in facsimile or transcript – may infringe copyright.

1 Making copies from microfilms

The PRO has no objection to the reproduction of limited quantities of hard copy print from microfilms of the census returns held by local libraries, family history societies, and other non-profit-making organisations. It is perfectly acceptable for holders of such microfilms to supply, for example:

(a) single copies of isolated pages to individuals for purposes of research or private study

(b) single copies of consecutive pages covering an area of one complete parish, to local or family history societies or individuals, for purposes of academic or other non-commercial research including the compilation of indexes to the returns

(c) multiple copies of isolated or small numbers of consecutive pages, to teachers or lecturers, for use with classes in schools or as part of a higher or adult education programme

2 Publishing facsimiles and transcripts of the returns

No permission need be sought for publication of extracts from the returns in transcript. Requests for permission to publish parts of the returns in facsimile should be addressed to the Image Library at the PRO, which will in most instances be able to give permission for the project on payment of a reproduction fee.

Requests for permission to publish should be made in writing, and should always include full details of the proposed publication, and the PRO document reference(s) of the returns concerned. These references are clearly visible on all microfilm copies of the census returns.

The published version, whether transcript or facsimile, should always carry an acknowledgement of the PRO as custodian of the original documents together with the document reference.

Grace Darling (HO 107/318, book 4, f. 3, p. 1)

3 Publishing indexes to the returns

Permission is not required for the publication of indexes to the returns.

4 The 1881 Project

Two distinct copyrights subsist in the indexes to the 1881 census. The data from the returns are Crown Copyright: copyright in the indexes themselves, including their arrangement and layout, belongs to the Corporation of the President, the Church of Jesus Christ of Latter-day Saints. Both copyright owners are happy that limited numbers of copies (both fiche and hard copy) should be made from the microfiche edition, in the quantities and for the purposes outlined in paragraph 1 above. Requests for permission to produce or obtain more extensive quantities of copies, or for permission to publish any portion of the indexes in facsimile or transcript, should be addressed in the first instance to the copyright officer of the Church.

Francis Kilvert, Clergyman and Schoolmaster (HO 107/1940, f. 444)

Appendix 4: Document references

Reference numbers are needed to identify specific documents, not just census returns, and have three component parts at the PRO. The first is the department code to the group of documents into which your particular document falls. This department code relates to the government department which transferred the document. In the case of the census this is HO (Home Office) for 1841 and 1851 and RG (Registrar General) for all other years.

The second part is a series number, since each group of documents is subdivided into series relating to different types of documents all being transferred from the same source. To cite an example, the series of the RG group are as follows: RG 1–3 are the indexes to the birth, marriage and death registers still held by the Office for National Statistics; RG 4 nonconformist registers (gathered in 1837); RG 5 certificates of Dr Williams' Library; RG 6 Quaker registers; RG 7 Fleet marriage registers; RG 8 unauthenticated nonconformist registers (gathered in 1857); RG 9 1861 census returns; RG 10 1871 census returns; RG 11 1881 census returns; RG 12 1891 census returns; RG 13 1901 census returns etc. RG 18 reference maps of registrar's districts, RG 19 correspondence and papers, RG 27 specimens of forms and documents and RG 30 reports and population abstracts, are some of the later series.

The third part of the reference is what is known as a piece number. This is simply an archival term for an individual item which may take many shapes and forms, but which when relating to the census means an enumerator's folder or in 1841 and 1851 a box of these folders.

To complete a reference add the particular folio number or numbers followed by either recto or verso, or a page number. See p. 45 for a fuller explanation.

These document references are universal in that they are present on a reel of census microfilm wherever you view it. However, if you are looking at the census away from the FRC or PRO in a local record office or family history library, you will not have the same finding aids to identify your part of the census in the same way. Other search rooms need to add any purchased microfilms to their own holdings. This means that a new reference consistent with their own referencing system is applied to any item purchased by them. Local record offices in particular may have also purchased copies of street indexes, where available, from the PRO, so that PRO references can be used in conjunction with their own system. Taking a PRO reference number to another record office may therefore necessitate an extra exercise before you can find your film. The local archivist or search room officer should be able to help you. Once you have found your place on the film you can refer back to it by the method described on p. 45. Similarly the local referencing system will not be intelligible away from its own collection, so you will need the PRO reference for what you wish to record to make it universally intelligible.

Charles H Spurgeon, Baptist Minister (RG 12/596, f. 102)

Appendix 5: FRC location map

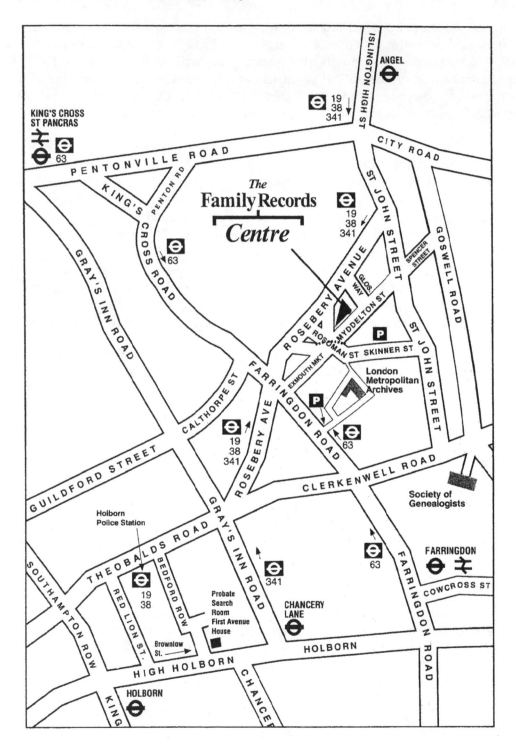

Charles Bowdler, Proctor (HO 107/678, book 4, f. 8, p. 10)

Appendix 6: FRC first floor plan

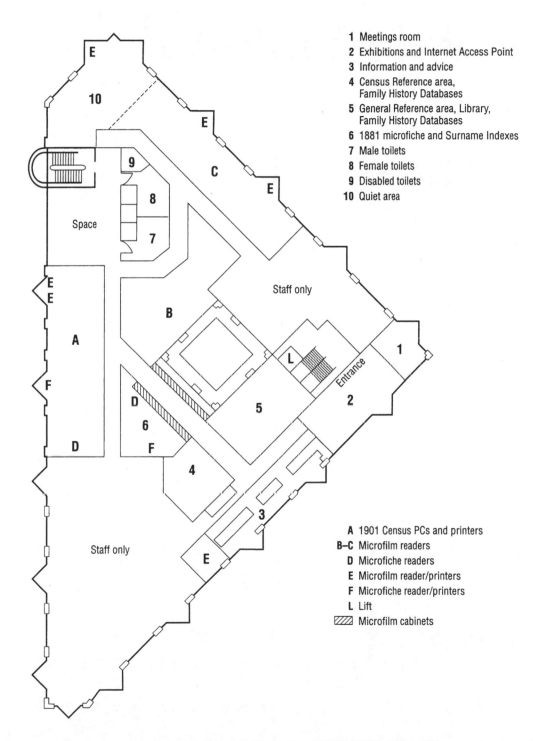

1 Meetings room
2 Exhibitions and Internet Access Point
3 Information and advice
4 Census Reference area,
 Family History Databases
5 General Reference area, Library,
 Family History Databases
6 1881 microfiche and Surname Indexes
7 Male toilets
8 Female toilets
9 Disabled toilets
10 Quiet area

A 1901 Census PCs and printers
B–C Microfilm readers
D Microfiche readers
E Microfilm reader/printers
F Microfiche reader/printers
L Lift
▨ Microfilm cabinets

Quaglinos Circus, in a Wooden Tent (RG 10/4685, f. 53, p. 43)

Appendix 7: Registration districts

London Division 1

1851 No.	1851	1861 No.	1861	1871 No.	1871	1881 No.	1881	1891 No.	1891	1901 No.	1901
	pt Kensington		pt Kensington		pt Kensington	1A	pt Kensington	1A	Paddington	1A	Paddington
1	Kensington	1	Kensington	1	Kensington	1B	Kensington	1B	Kensington	1B	Kensington
	pt Kensington		pt Kensington		pt Kensington	2	Fulham	2	Fulham	2	Fulham
2	Chelsea	2	Chelsea	2	Chelsea	3	Chelsea	3	Chelsea	3	Chelsea
3	St George Hanover Sq	3	St George Hanover Sq	3	St George Hanover Sq	4	St George Hanover Sq	4	St George Hanover Sq	4	St George Hanover Sq
4	Westminster	4	Westminster	4	Westminster	5	Westminster	5	Westminster	5	Westminster
5	St Martin in the Fields	5	St Martin in the Fields		pt Westminster		pt Westminster		pt Westminster		pt Westminster
6	St James Westminster	6	St James Westminster		pt Westminster		pt Westminster		pt Westminster		pt Westminster
7	Marylebone	7	Marylebone	5	Marylebone	6	Marylebone	6	Marylebone	6	Marylebone
8	Hampstead	8	Hampstead	6	Hampstead	7	Hampstead	7	Hampstead	7	Hampstead
9	Pancras	9	Pancras	7	Pancras	8	Pancras	8	Pancras	8	Pancras
10	Islington	10	Islington	8	Islington	9	Islington	9	Islington	9	Islington
11	Hackney	11	Hackney	9	Hackney	10	Hackney	10	Hackney	10	Hackney
12	St Giles	12	St Giles	10	St Giles	11	St Giles	11	St Giles	11	St Giles
13	Strand	13	Strand	11	Strand	12	Strand	12	Strand	12	Strand
14	Holborn	14	Holborn	12	Holborn	13	Holborn	13	Holborn	13	Holborn
15	Clerkenwell	15	Clerkenwell		pt Holborn		pt Holborn		pt Holborn		pt Holborn
16	St Luke	16	St Luke		pt Holborn		pt Holborn		pt Holborn		pt Holborn
17	E London	17	E London		pt London City		pt London City		pt London City		pt London City
18	W London	18	W London		pt London City		pt London City		pt London City		pt London City
19	London City	19	London City	13	London City	14	London City	14	London City	14	London City
20	Shoreditch	20	Shoreditch	14	Shoreditch	15	Shoreditch	15	Shoreditch	15	Shoreditch
21	Bethnal Green	21	Bethnal Green	15	Bethnal Green	16	Bethnal Green	16	Bethnal Green	16	Bethnal Green
22	Whitechapel	22	Whitechapel	16	Whitechapel	17	Whitechapel	17	Whitechapel	17	Whitechapel
23	St George in the East	23	St George in the East	17	St George in the East	18	St George in the East	18	St George in the East	18	St George in the East
24A	Stepney	24A	Stepney	18	Stepney	19	Stepney	19	Stepney	19	Stepney
	pt Stepney										
24B	Mile End Old Town	24B	Mile End Old Town	19	Mile End Old Town	20	Mile End Old Town	20	Mile End Old Town	20	Mile End Old Town
25	Poplar	25	Poplar	20	Poplar	21	Poplar	21	Poplar	21	Poplar

1851		1861		1871		1881		1891		1901	
26	St Saviour Southwark	26	St Saviour Southwark	21	St Saviour Southwark	22	St Saviour Southwark	22	St Saviour Southwark	22	St Saviour Southwark
27	St Olave Southwark	27	St Olave Southwark	22	St Olave Southwark	23	St Olave Southwark	23	St Olave Southwark	23	St Olave Southwark
28	Bermondsey	28	Bermondsey		pt St Olave		pt St Olave		pt St Olave		pt St Olave
29	St George Southwark	29	St George Southwark		pt St Saviour		pt St Saviour		pt St Saviour		pt St Saviour
30	Newington	30	Newington		pt St Saviour		pt St Saviour		pt St Saviour		pt St Saviour
31	Lambeth	31	Lambeth	23	Lambeth	24	Lambeth	24	Lambeth	24	Lambeth
32	Wandsworth	32	Wandsworth	24	Wandsworth	25	Wandsworth	25	Wandsworth	25	Wandsworth
33	Camberwell	33	Camberwell	25	Camberwell	26	Camberwell	26	Camberwell	26	Camberwell
34	Rotherhithe	34	Rotherhithe		pt St Olave		pt St Olave		pt St Olave		pt St Olave
35	Greenwich	35	Greenwich	26	Greenwich	27	Greenwich	27	Greenwich	27	Greenwich
36	Lewisham	36	Lewisham	27	Lewisham	28	Lewisham	28	Lewisham	28	Lewisham
	pt Greenwich		pt Greenwich	28	Woolwich	29	Woolwich	29	Woolwich	29	Woolwich
Surrey											
37	Epsom	37	Epsom	29	Epsom	30	Epsom	30	Epsom	30	Epsom
38	Chertsey	38	Chertsey	30	Chertsey	31	Chertsey	31	Chertsey	31	Chertsey
39	Guildford	39	Guildford	31	Guildford	32	Guildford	32	Guildford	32	Guildford
40	Farnham	40	Farnham	32	Farnham	33	Farnham	33	Farnham	33	Farnham
41	Farnborough	41	Farnborough		pt Hartley Wintney (Hants)		pt Hartley Wintney (Hants)		pt Hartley Wintney (Hants)		pt Hartley Wintney (Hants)
42	Hambledon	42	Hambledon	33	Hambledon	34	Hambledon	34	Hambledon	34	Hambledon
43	Dorking	43	Dorking	34	Dorking	35	Dorking	35	Dorking	35	Dorking
44	Reigate	44	Reigate	35	Reigate	36	Reigate	36	Reigate	36	Reigate
45	Godstone	45	Godstone	36	Godstone	37	Godstone	37	Godstone	37	Godstone
46	Croydon	46	Croydon	37	Croydon	38	Croydon	38	Croydon	38	Croydon
47	Kingston	47	Kingston	38	Kingston	39	Kingston	39	Kingston	39	Kingston
48	Richmond	48	Richmond	39	Richmond	40	Richmond	40	Richmond	40	Richmond
Kent											
49	Bromley	49	Bromley	40	Bromley	41	Bromley	41	Bromley	41	Bromley
50	Dartford	50	Dartford	41	Dartford	42	Dartford	42	Dartford	42	Dartford
51	Gravesend	51	Gravesend	42	Gravesend	43	Gravesend	43	Gravesend	43	Gravesend
52	North Aylesford	52	North Aylesford	43	North Aylesford	44	North Aylesford	44	Strood	44	Strood

1851	1861	1871	1881	1891	1901
53 Hoo	53 Hoo	44 Hoo	45 Hoo	45 Hoo	45 Hoo
54 Medway	54 Medway	45 Medway	46 Medway	46 Medway	46 Medway
55 Malling	55 Malling	46 Malling	47 Malling	47 Malling	47 Malling
56 Sevenoaks	56 Sevenoaks	47 Sevenoaks	48 Sevenoaks	48 Sevenoaks	48 Sevenoaks
57 Tonbridge	57 Tonbridge	48 Tonbridge	49 Tonbridge	49 Tonbridge	49 Tonbridge
58 Maidstone	58 Maidstone	49 Maidstone	50 Maidstone	50 Maidstone	50 Maidstone
59 Hollingbourne	59 Hollingbourne	50 Hollingbourne	51 Hollingbourne	51 Hollingbourne	51 Hollingbourne
60 Cranbrook	60 Cranbrook	51 Cranbrook	52 Cranbrook	52 Cranbrook	52 Cranbrook
61 Tenterden	61 Tenterden	52 Tenterden	53 Tenterden	53 Tenterden	53 Tenterden
62 West Ashford	62 West Ashford	53 West Ashford	54 West Ashford	54 West Ashford	54 West Ashford
63 East Ashford	63 East Ashford	54 East Ashford	55 East Ashford	55 East Ashford	55 East Ashford
64 Bridge	64 Bridge	55 Bridge	56 Bridge	56 Bridge	56 Bridge
65 Canterbury	65 Canterbury	56 Canterbury	57 Canterbury	57 Canterbury	57 Canterbury
66 Blean	66 Blean	57 Blean	58 Blean	58 Blean	58 Blean
67 Faversham	67 Faversham	58 Faversham	59 Faversham	59 Faversham	59 Faversham
68 Milton	68 Milton	59 Milton	60 Milton	60 Milton	60 Milton
69 Sheppey	69 Sheppey	60 Sheppey	61 Sheppey	61 Sheppey	61 Sheppey
70 Thanet	70 Thanet	61 Thanet	62 Thanet	62 Thanet	62 Thanet
71 Eastry	71 Eastry	62 Eastry	63 Eastry	63 Eastry	63 Eastry
72 Dover	72 Dover	63 Dover	64 Dover	64 Dover	64 Dover
73 Elham	73 Elham	64 Elham	65 Elham	65 Elham	65 Elham
74 Romney Marsh	74 Romney Marsh	65 Romney Marsh	66 Romney Marsh	66 Romney Marsh	66 Romney Marsh

Sussex

1851	1861	1871	1881	1891	1901
75 Rye	75 Rye	66 Rye	67 Rye	67 Rye	67 Rye
76 Hastings	76 Hastings	67 Hastings	68 Hastings	68 Hastings	68 Hastings
77 Battle	77 Battle	68 Battle	69 Battle	69 Battle	69 Battle
78 Eastbourne	78 Eastbourne	69 Eastbourne	70 Eastbourne	70 Eastbourne	70 Eastbourne
79 Hailsham	79 Hailsham	70 Hailsham	71 Hailsham	71 Hailsham	71 Hailsham
80 Ticehurst	80 Ticehurst	71 Ticehurst	72 Ticehurst	72 Ticehurst	72 Ticehurst
81 Uckfield	81 Uckfield	72 Uckfield	73 Uckfield	73 Uckfield	73 Uckfield
82 East Grinstead	82 East Grinstead	73 East Grinstead	74 East Grinstead	74 East Grinstead	74 East Grinstead

1851	1861	1871	1881	1891	1901
83 Cuckfield	83 Cuckfield	74 Cuckfield	75 Cuckfield	75 Cuckfield	75 Cuckfield
84 Lewes	84 Lewes	75 Lewes	76 Lewes	76 Lewes	76 Lewes
85 Brighton	85 Brighton	76 Brighton	77 Brighton	77 Brighton	77 Brighton
86 Steyning	86 Steyning	77 Steyning	78 Steyning	78 Steyning	78 Steyning
87 Horsham	87 Horsham	78 Horsham	79 Horsham	79 Horsham	79 Horsham
88 Petworth	88 Petworth	79 Petworth	80 Petworth	80 Petworth	80 Petworth
89 Thakeham	89 Thakeham	80 Thakeham	81 Thakeham	81 Thakeham	81 Thakeham
pt Worthing	pt Worthing	81 East Preston	82 East Preston	82 East Preston	82 East Preston
90 Worthing	90 Worthing	pt East Preston	pt East Preston	pt East Preston	pt East Preston
91 Westhampnett	91 Westhampnett	82 Westhampnett	83 Westhampnett	83 Westhampnett	83 Westhampnett
92 Chichester	92 Chichester	33 Chichester	84 Chichester	84 Chichester	84 Chichester
93 Midhurst	93 Midhurst	84 Midhurst	85 Midhurst	85 Midhurst	85 Midhurst
94 Westbourne	94 Westbourne	85 Westbourne	86 Westbourne	86 Westbourne	86 Westbourne

Hampshire

1851	1861	1871	1881	1891	1901
95 Havant	95 Havant	86 Havant	87 Havant	87 Havant	87 Havant
96 Portsea Island	96 Portsea Island	87 Portsea Island	88 Portsea Island	88 Portsea Island	88 Portsmouth
97 Alverstoke	97 Alverstoke	88 Alverstoke	89 Alverstoke	89 Alverstoke	89 Alverstoke
98 Fareham	98 Fareham	89 Fareham	90 Fareham	90 Fareham	90 Fareham
99 Isle of Wight	99 Isle of Wight	90 Isle of Wight	91 Isle of Wight	91 Isle of Wight	91 Isle of Wight
100 Lymington	100 Lymington	91 Lymington	92 Lymington	92 Lymington	92 Lymington
101 Christchurch	101 Christchurch	92 Christchurch	93 Christchurch	93 Christchurch	93 Christchurch
102 Ringwood	102 Ringwood	93 Ringwood	94 Ringwood	94 Ringwood	94 Ringwood
103 Fordingbridge	103 Fordingbridge	94 Fordingbridge	95 Fordingbridge	95 Fordingbridge	95 Fordingbridge
104 New Forest	104 New Forest	95 New Forest	96 New Forest	96 New Forest	96 New Forest
105 Southampton	105 Southampton	96 Southampton	97 Southampton	97 Southampton	97 Southampton
106 South Stoneham	106 South Stoneham	97 South Stoneham	98 South Stoneham	98 South Stoneham	98 South Stoneham
107 Romsey	107 Romsey	98 Romsey	99 Romsey	99 Romsey	99 Romsey
108 Stockbridge	108 Stockbridge	99 Stockbridge	100 Stockbridge	100 Stockbridge	100 Stockbridge
109 Winchester	109 Winchester	100 Winchester	101 Winchester	101 Winchester	101 Winchester
110 Droxford	110 Droxford	101 Droxford	102 Droxford	102 Droxford	102 Droxford
111 Catherington	111 Catherington	102 Catherington	103 Catherington	103 Catherington	103 Catherington

1851	1861	1871	1881	1891	1901
112 Petersfield	112 Petersfield	103 Petersfield	104 Petersfield	104 Petersfield	104 Petersfield
113 Alresford	113 Alresford	104 Alresford	105 Alresford	105 Alresford	105 Alresford
114 Alton	114 Alton	105 Alton	106 Alton	106 Alton	106 Alton
115 Hartley Wintney	115 Hartley Wintney	106 Hartley Wintney	107 Hartley Wintney	107 Hartley Wintney	107 Hartley Wintney
116 Basingstoke	116 Basingstoke	107 Basingstoke	108 Basingstoke	108 Basingstoke	108 Basingstoke
117 Whitchurch	117 Whitchurch	108 Whitchurch	109 Whitchurch	109 Whitchurch	109 Whitchurch
118 Andover	118 Andover	109 Andover	110 Andover	110 Andover	110 Andover
119 Kingsclere	119 Kingsclere	110 Kingsclere	111 Kingsclere	111 Kingsclere	111 Kingsclere

Berkshire

1851	1861	1871	1881	1891	1901
120 Newbury	120 Newbury	111 Newbury	112 Newbury	112 Newbury	112 Newbury
121 Hungerford	121 Hungerford	112 Hungerford	113 Hungerford	113 Hungerford	113 Hungerford
122 Faringdon	122 Faringdon	113 Faringdon	114 Faringdon	114 Faringdon	114 Faringdon
123 Abingdon	123 Abingdon	114 Abingdon	115 Abingdon	115 Abingdon	115 Abingdon
124 Wantage	124 Wantage	115 Wantage	116 Wantage	116 Wantage	116 Wantage
125 Wallingford	125 Wallingford	116 Wallingford	117 Wallingford	117 Wallingford	117 Wallingford
126 Bradfield	126 Bradfield	117 Bradfield	118 Bradfield	118 Bradfield	118 Bradfield
127 Reading	127 Reading	118 Reading	119 Reading	119 Reading	119 Reading
128 Wokingham	128 Wokingham	119 Wokingham	120 Wokingham	120 Wokingham	120 Wokingham
129 Cookham	129 Cookham	120 Cookham	121 Cookham	121 Cookham	121 Maidenhead
130 Easthampstead	130 Easthampstead	121 Easthampstead	122 Easthampstead	122 Easthampstead	122 Easthampstead
131 Windsor	131 Windsor	122 Windsor	123 Windsor	123 Windsor	123 Windsor

Middlesex

1851	1861	1871	1881	1891	1901
132 Staines	132 Staines	123 Staines	124 Staines	124 Staines	124 Staines
133 Uxbridge	133 Uxbridge	124 Uxbridge	125 Uxbridge	125 Uxbridge	125 Uxbridge
134 Brentford	134 Brentford	125 Brentford	126 Brentford	126 Brentford	126 Brentford
135 Hendon	135 Hendon	126 Hendon	127 Hendon	127 Hendon	127 Hendon
136 Barnet	136 Barnet	127 Barnet	128 Barnet	128 Barnet	128 Barnet
137 Edmonton	137 Edmonton	128 Edmonton	129 Edmonton	129 Edmonton	129 Edmonton

Hertfordshire

1851	1861	1871	1881	1891	1901
138 Ware	138 Ware	129 Ware	130 Ware	130 Ware	130 Ware
139 Bishops Stortford	139 Bishops Stortford	130 Bishops Stortford	131 Bishops Stortford	131 Bishops Stortford	131 Bishops Stortford

District	1851	1861	1871	1881	1891	1901
Royston	140	140	131	132	132	132
Hitchin	141	141	132	133	133	133
Hertford	142	142	133	134	134	134
Hatfield	143	143	134	135	135	135
St Albans	144	144	135	136	136	136
Watford	145	145	136	137	137	137
Hemel Hempstead	146	146	137	138	138	138
Berkhamsted	147	147	138	139	139	139
Buckinghamshire						
Amersham	148	148	139	140	140	140
Eton	149	149	140	141	141	141
Wycombe	150	150	141	142	142	142
Aylesbury	151	151	142	143	143	143
Winslow	152	152	143	144	144	144
Newport Pagnell	153	153	144	145	145	145
Buckingham	154	154	145	146	146	146
Oxfordshire						
Henley	155	155	146	147	147	147
Thame	156	156	147	148	148	148
Headington	157	157	148	149	149	149
Oxford	158	158	149	150	150	150
Bicester	159	159	150	151	151	151
Woodstock	160	160	151	152	152	152
Witney	161	161	152	153	153	153
Chipping Norton	162	162	153	154	154	154
Banbury	163	163	154	155	155	155
Northamptonshire						
Brackley	164	164	155	156	156	156
Towcester	165	165	156	157	157	157
Potterspury	166	166	157	158	158	158
Hardingstone	167	167	158	159	159	159

Place	1851	1861	1871	1881	1891	1901
Northampton	168	168	159	160	160	160
Daventry	169	169	160	161	161	161
Brixworth	170	170	161	162	162	162
Wellingborough	171	171	162	163	163	163
Kettering	172	172	163	164	164	164
Thrapston	173	173	164	165	165	165
Oundle	174	174	165	166	166	166
Peterborough	175	175	166	167	167	167
Huntingdonshire						
Huntingdon	176	176	167	168	168	168
St Ives	177	177	168	169	169	169
St Neots	178	178	169	170	170	170
Bedfordshire						
Bedford	179	179	170	171	171	171
Biggleswade	180	180	171	172	172	172
Ampthill	181	181	172	173	173	173
Woburn	182	182	173	174	174	174
Leighton Buzzard	183	183	174	175	175	175
Luton	184	184	175	176	176	176
Cambridgeshire						
Caxton	185	185	176	177	177	177
Chesterton	186	186	177	178	178	178
Cambridge	187	187	178	179	179	179
Linton	188	188	179	180	180	180
Newmarket	189	189	180	181	181	181
Ely	190	190	181	182	182	182
North Witchford	191	191	182	183	183	183
Whittlesey	192	192	183	184	184	184
Wisbech	193	193	184	185	185	185
Essex						
West Ham	194	194	185	186	186	186

District	1851	1861	1871	1881	1891	1901
Epping	195	195	186	187	187	187
Ongar	196	196	187	188	188	188
Romford	197	197	188	189	189	189
Orsett	198	198	189	190	190	190
Billericay	199	199	190	191	191	191
Chelmsford	200	200	191	192	192	192
Rochford	201	201	192	193	193	193
Maldon	202	202	193	194	194	194
Tendring	203	203	194	195	195	195
Colchester	204	204	195	196	196	196
Lexden	205	205	196	197	197	197
Witham / pt Braintree	206 Witham	206 Witham	197 Witham	pt Braintree	pt Braintree	pt Braintree
Halstead	207	207	198	198	198	198
Braintree	208	208	199	199	199	199
Dunmow	209	209	200	200	200	200
Saffron Walden	210	210	201	201	201	201

Suffolk

District	1851	1861	1871	1881	1891	1901
Risbridge	211	211	202	202	202	202
Sudbury	212	212	203	203	203	203
Cosford	213	213	204	204	204	204
Thingoe	214	214	205	205	205	205
Bury St Edmunds	215	215	206	206	206	206
Mildenhall	216	216	207	207	207	207
Stow	217	217	208	208	208	208
Hartismere	218	218	209	209	209	209
Hoxne	219	219	210	210	210	210
Bosmere	220	220	211	211	211	211
Samford	221	221	212	212	212	212
Ipswich	222	222	213	213	213	213
Woodbridge	223	223	214	214	214	214
Plomesgate	224	224	215	215	215	215

1851	1861	1871	1881	1891	1901
225 Blything	225 Blything	216 Blything	216 Blything	216 Blything	216 Blything
226 Wangford	226 Wangford	217 Wangford	217 Wangford	217 Wangford	217 Wangford
227 Mutford	227 Mutford	218 Mutford	218 Mutford	218 Mutford	218 Mutford

Norfolk

1851	1861	1871	1881	1891	1901
228 Yarmouth	228 Yarmouth	219 Yarmouth	219 Yarmouth	219 Yarmouth	219 Yarmouth
229 Flegg	229 Flegg	220 Flegg	220 Flegg	220 Flegg	220 Flegg
230 Tunstead	230 Tunstead	221 Smallburgh	221 Smallburgh	221 Smallburgh	221 Smallburgh
231 Erpingham	231 Erpingham	222 Erpingham	222 Erpingham	222 Erpingham	222 Erpingham
232 Aylsham	232 Aylsham	223 Aylsham	223 Aylsham	223 Aylsham	223 Aylsham
233 St Faith's	233 St Faith's	224 St Faith's	224 St Faith's	224 St Faith's	224 St Faith's
234 Norwich	234 Norwich	225 Norwich	225 Norwich	225 Norwich	225 Norwich
235 Forehoe	235 Forehoe	226 Forehoe	226 Forehoe	226 Forehoe	226 Forehoe
236 Henstead	236 Henstead	227 Henstead	227 Henstead	227 Henstead	227 Henstead
237 Blofield	237 Blofield	228 Blofield	228 Blofield	228 Blofield	228 Blofield
238 Loddon	238 Loddon	229 Loddon	229 Loddon	229 Loddon	229 Loddon
239 Depwade	239 Depwade	230 Depwade	230 Depwade	230 Depwade	230 Depwade
240 Guiltcross	240 Guiltcross	231 Guiltcross	231 Guiltcross	231 Guiltcross	231 Guiltcross
241 Wayland	241 Wayland	232 Wayland	232 Wayland	232 Wayland	232 Wayland
242 Mitford	242 Mitford	233 Mitford	233 Mitford	233 Mitford	233 Mitford
243 Walsingham	243 Walsingham	234 Walsingham	234 Walsingham	234 Walsingham	234 Walsingham
244 Docking	244 Docking	235 Docking	235 Docking	235 Docking	235 Docking
245 Freebridge Lynn	245 Freebridge Lynn	236 Freebridge Lynn	236 Freebridge Lynn	236 Freebridge Lynn	236 Freebridge Lynn
246 King's Lynn	246 King's Lynn	237 King's Lynn	237 King's Lynn	237 King's Lynn	237 King's Lynn
247 Downham	247 Downham	238 Downham	238 Downham	238 Downham	238 Downham
248 Swaffham	248 Swaffham	239 Swaffham	239 Swaffham	239 Swaffham	239 Swaffham
249 Thetford	249 Thetford	240 Thetford	240 Thetford	240 Thetford	240 Thetford

Wiltshire

1851	1861	1871	1881	1891	1901
250 Highworth	250 Highworth	241 Highworth	241 Highworth	241 Highworth	241 Swindon
251 Cricklade	251 Cricklade	242 Cricklade	242 Cricklade	242 Cricklade	242 Cricklade
252 Malmesbury	252 Malmesbury	243 Malmesbury	243 Malmesbury	243 Malmesbury	243 Malmesbury
253 Chippenham	253 Chippenham	244 Chippenham	244 Chippenham	244 Chippenham	244 Chippenham

1851	1861	1871	1881	1891	1901
254 Calne	254 Calne	245 Calne	245 Calne	245 Calne	245 Calne
255 Marlborough	255 Marlborough	246 Marlborough	246 Marlborough	246 Marlborough	246 Marlborough
256 Devizes	256 Devizes	247 Devizes	247 Devizes	247 Devizes	247 Devizes
257 Melksham	257 Melksham	248 Melksham	248 Melksham	248 Melksham	248 Melksham
258 Bradford on Avon	258 Bradford on Avon	249 Bradford on Avon	249 Bradford on Avon	249 Bradford on Avon	249 Bradford on Avon
259 Westbury	259 Westbury	250 Westbury	250 Westbury	250 Westbury	250 Westbury
260 Warminster	260 Warminster	251 Warminster	251 Warminster	251 Warminster	251 Warminster
261 Pewsey	261 Pewsey	252 Pewsey	252 Pewsey	252 Pewsey	252 Pewsey
262 Amesbury	262 Amesbury	253 Amesbury	253 Amesbury	253 Amesbury	253 Amesbury
263 Alderbury	263 Alderbury	254 Alderbury	254 Alderbury	254 Alderbury	pt Salisbury
264 Salisbury	264 Salisbury	pt Alderbury	pt Alderbury	pt Alderbury	254 Salisbury
265 Wilton	265 Wilton	255 Wilton	255 Wilton	255 Wilton	255 Wilton
266 Tisbury	266 Tisbury	256 Tisbury	256 Tisbury	256 Tisbury	256 Tisbury
267 Mere	267 Mere	257 Mere	257 Mere	257 Mere	257 Mere
Dorset					
268 Shaftesbury	268 Shaftesbury	258 Shaftesbury	258 Shaftesbury	258 Shaftesbury	258 Shaftesbury
269 Sturminster	269 Sturminster	259 Sturminster	259 Sturminster	259 Sturminster	259 Sturminster
270 Blandford	270 Blandford	260 Blandford	260 Blandford	260 Blandford	260 Blandford
271 Wimborne	271 Wimborne	261 Wimborne	261 Wimborne	261 Wimborne	261 Wimborne
272 Poole	272 Poole	262 Poole	262 Poole	262 Poole	262 Poole
273 Wareham	273 Wareham	263 Wareham	263 Wareham	263 Wareham	263 Wareham
274 Weymouth	274 Weymouth	264 Weymouth	264 Weymouth	264 Weymouth	264 Weymouth
275 Dorchester	275 Dorchester	265 Dorchester	265 Dorchester	265 Dorchester	265 Dorchester
276 Sherborne	276 Sherborne	266 Sherborne	266 Sherborne	266 Sherborne	266 Sherborne
277 Beaminster	277 Beaminster	267 Beaminster	267 Beaminster	267 Beaminster	267 Beaminster
278 Bridport	278 Bridport	268 Bridport	268 Bridport	268 Bridport	268 Bridport
Devonshire					
279 Axminster	279 Axminster	269 Axminster	269 Axminster	269 Axminster	269 Axminster
280 Honiton	280 Honiton	270 Honiton	270 Honiton	270 Honiton	270 Honiton
281 St Thomas	281 St Thomas	271 St Thomas	271 St Thomas	271 St Thomas	271 St Thomas
282 Exeter	282 Exeter	272 Exeter	272 Exeter	272 Exeter	272 Exeter

1851		1861		1871		1881		1891		1901	
283	Newton Abbot	283	Newton Abbot	273	Newton Abbot	273	Newton Abbot	273	Newton Abbot	273	Newton Abbot
284	Totnes	284	Totnes	274	Totnes	274	Totnes	274	Totnes	274	Totnes
285	Kingsbridge	285	Kingsbridge	275	Kingsbridge	275	Kingsbridge	275	Kingsbridge	275	Kingsbridge
286	Plympton St Mary	286	Plympton St Mary	276	Plympton St Mary	276	Plympton St Mary	276	Plympton St Mary	276	Plympton St Mary
287	Plymouth	287	Plymouth	277	Plymouth	277	Plymouth	277	Plymouth	277	Plymouth
288	East Stonehouse	288	East Stonehouse	278	East Stonehouse	278	East Stonehouse	278	East Stonehouse	278	East Stonehouse
289	Stoke Damerel	289	Stoke Damerel	279	Stoke Damerel	279	Stoke Damerel	279	Stoke Damerel	279	Devonport
290	Tavistock	290	Tavistock	280	Tavistock	280	Tavistock	280	Tavistock	280	Tavistock
291	Okehampton	291	Okehampton	281	Okehampton	281	Okehampton	281	Okehampton	281	Okehampton
292	Crediton	292	Crediton	282	Crediton	282	Crediton	282	Crediton	282	Crediton
293	Tiverton	293	Tiverton	283	Tiverton	283	Tiverton	283	Tiverton	283	Tiverton
294	South Molton	294	South Molton	284	South Molton	284	South Molton	284	South Molton	284	South Molton
295	Barnstaple	295	Barnstaple	285	Barnstaple	285	Barnstaple	285	Barnstaple	285	Barnstaple
296	Torrington	296	Torrington	286	Torrington	286	Torrington	286	Torrington	286	Torrington
297	Bideford	297	Bideford	287	Bideford	287	Bideford	287	Bideford	287	Bideford
298	Holsworthy	298	Holsworthy	288	Holsworthy	288	Holsworthy	288	Holsworthy	288	Holsworthy

Cornwall

1851		1861		1871		1881		1891		1901	
299	Stratton	299	Stratton	289	Stratton	289	Stratton	289	Stratton	289	Stratton
300	Camelford	300	Camelford	290	Camelford	290	Camelford	290	Camelford	290	Camelford
301	Launceston	301	Launceston	291	Launceston	291	Launceston	291	Launceston	291	Launceston
302	St Germans	302	St Germans	292	St Germans	292	St Germans	292	St Germans	292	St Germans
303	Liskeard	303	Liskeard	293	Liskeard	293	Liskeard	293	Liskeard	293	Liskeard
304	Bodmin	304	Bodmin	294	Bodmin	294	Bodmin	294	Bodmin	294	Bodmin
305	St Columb	305	St Columb	295	St Columb	295	St Columb	295	St Columb	295	St Columb
306	St Austell	306	St Austell	296	St Austell	296	St Austell	296	St Austell	296	St Austell
307	Truro	307	Truro	297	Truro	297	Truro	297	Truro	297	Truro
308	Falmouth	308	Falmouth	298	Falmouth	298	Falmouth	298	Falmouth	298	Falmouth
309	Helston	309	Helston	299	Helston	299	Helston	299	Helston	299	Helston
310	Redruth	310	Redruth	300	Redruth	300	Redruth	300	Redruth	300	Redruth
311	Penzance	311	Penzance	301	Penzance	301	Penzance	301	Penzance	301	Penzance
312	Scilly Isles	312	Scilly Isles	302	Scilly Isles	302	Scilly Isles	302	Scilly Isles	302	Scilly Isles

1851	1861	1871	1881	1891	1901
Somerset					
313 Williton	313A Williton	303 Williton	303 Williton	303 Williton	303 Williton
pt Tiverton	313B Dulverton	304 Dulverton	304 Dulverton	304 Dulverton	304 Dulverton
314 Wellington	314 Wellington	305 Wellington	305 Wellington	305 Wellington	305 Wellington
315 Taunton	315 Taunton	306 Taunton	306 Taunton	306 Taunton	306 Taunton
316 Bridgwater	316 Bridgwater	307 Bridgwater	307 Bridgwater	307 Bridgwater	307 Bridgwater
317 Langport	317 Langport	308 Langport	308 Langport	308 Langport	308 Langport
318 Chard	318 Chard	309 Chard	309 Chard	309 Chard	309 Chard
319 Yeovil	319 Yeovil	310 Yeovil	310 Yeovil	310 Yeovil	310 Yeovil
320 Wincanton	320 Wincanton	311 Wincanton	311 Wincanton	311 Wincanton	311 Wincanton
321 Frome	321 Frome	312 Frome	312 Frome	312 Frome	312 Frome
322 Shepton Mallet	322 Shepton Mallet	313 Shepton Mallet	313 Shepton Mallet	313 Shepton Mallet	313 Shepton Mallet
323 Wells	323 Wells	314 Wells	314 Wells	314 Wells	314 Wells
324 Axbridge	324 Axbridge	315 Axbridge	315 Axbridge	315 Axbridge	315 Axbridge
325 Clutton	325 Clutton	316 Clutton	316 Clutton	316 Clutton	316 Clutton
326 Bath	326 Bath	317 Bath	317 Bath	317 Bath	317 Bath
327 Keynsham	327 Keynsham	318 Keynsham	318 Keynsham	318 Keynsham	318 Keynsham
328 Bedminster	328 Bedminster	319 Bedminster	319 Bedminster	319 Bedminster	319 Long Ashton
Gloucestershire					
329 Bristol	329 Bristol	320 Bristol	320 Bristol	320 Bristol	320 Bristol
330 Clifton	330 Clifton	321 Clifton	321 Barton Regis	321 Barton Regis	321 Barton Regis
331 Chipping Sodbury	331 Chipping Sodbury	322 Chipping Sodbury	322 Chipping Sodbury	322 Chipping Sodbury	322 Chipping Sodbury
332 Thornbury	332 Thornbury	323 Thornbury	323 Thornbury	323 Thornbury	323 Thornbury
333 Dursley	333 Dursley	324 Dursley	324 Dursley	324 Dursley	324 Dursley
334 Westbury on Severn	334 Westbury on Severn	325 Westbury on Severn	325 Westbury on Severn	325 Westbury on Severn	325 Westbury on Severn
335 Newent	335 Newent	326 Newent	326 Newent	326 Newent	326 Newent
336 Gloucester	336 Gloucester	327 Gloucester	327 Gloucester	327 Gloucester	327 Gloucester
337 Wheatenhurst	337 Wheatenhurst	328 Wheatenhurst	328 Wheatenhurst	328 Wheatenhurst	328 Wheatenhurst
338 Stroud	338 Stroud	329 Stroud	329 Stroud	329 Stroud	329 Stroud
339 Tetbury	339 Tetbury	330 Tetbury	330 Tetbury	330 Tetbury	330 Tetbury
340 Cirencester	340 Cirencester	331 Cirencester	331 Cirencester	331 Cirencester	331 Cirencester

1851		1861		1871		1881		1891		1901	
341	Northleach	341	Northleach	332	Northleach	332	Northleach	332	Northleach	332	Northleach
342	Stow on the Wold	342	Stow on the Wold	333	Stow on the Wold	333	Stow on the Wold	333	Stow on the Wold	333	Stow on the Wold
343	Winchcomb	343	Winchcomb	334	Winchcomb	334	Winchcomb	334	Winchcomb	334	Winchcomb
344	Cheltenham	344	Cheltenham	335	Cheltenham	335	Cheltenham	335	Cheltenham	335	Cheltenham
345	Tewkesbury	345	Tewkesbury	336	Tewkesbury	336	Tewkesbury	336	Tewkesbury	336	Tewkesbury

Herefordshire

1851		1861		1871		1881		1891		1901	
346	Ledbury	346	Ledbury	337	Ledbury	337	Ledbury	337	Ledbury	337	Ledbury
347	Ross	347	Ross	338	Ross	338	Ross	338	Ross	338	Ross
348	Hereford	348	Hereford	339	Hereford	339	Hereford	339	Hereford	339	Hereford
349	Weobly	349	Weobley	340	Weobley	340	Weobley	340	Weobley	340	Weobley
350	Bromyard	350	Bromyard	341	Bromyard	341	Bromyard	341	Bromyard	341	Bromyard
351	Leominster	351	Leominster	342	Leominster	342	Leominster	342	Leominster	342	Leominster
	pt Presteigne		pt Presteigne	343	Kington	343	Kington	343	Kington	343	Kington

Shropshire

1851		1861		1871		1881		1891		1901	
352	Ludlow	352	Ludlow	344	Ludlow	344	Ludlow	344	Ludlow	344	Ludlow
353	Clun	353	Clun	345	Clun	345	Clun	345	Clun	345	Clun
354	Church Stretton	354	Church Stretton	346	Church Stretton	346	Church Stretton	346	Church Stretton	346	Church Stretton
355	Cleobury Mortimer	355	Cleobury Mortimer	347	Cleobury Mortimer	347	Cleobury Mortimer	347	Cleobury Mortimer	347	Cleobury Mortimer
356	Bridgnorth	356	Bridgnorth	348	Bridgnorth	348	Bridgnorth	348	Bridgnorth	348	Bridgnorth
357	Shifnal	357	Shifnal	349	Shifnal	349	Shifnal	349	Shifnal	349	Shifnal
358	Madeley	358	Madeley	350	Madeley	350	Madeley	350	Madeley	350	Madeley
359	Atcham	359	Atcham	351	Atcham	351	Atcham	351	Atcham	351	Atcham
360	Shrewsbury	360	Shrewsbury	352	Shrewsbury		pt Atcham		pt Atcham		pt Atcham
361	Oswestry	361	Oswestry	353	Oswestry	352	Oswestry	352	Oswestry	352	Oswestry
362	Ellesmere	362	Ellesmere	354	Ellesmere	353	Ellesmere	353	Ellesmere	353	Ellesmere
363	Wem	363A	Wem	355	Wem	354	Wem	354	Wem	354	Wem
	pt Wem	363B	Whitchurch	356	Whitchurch	355	Whitchurch	355	Whitchurch	355	Whitchurch
364	Market Drayton	364	Market Drayton	357	Market Drayton	356	Market Drayton	356	Market Drayton	356	Market Drayton
365	Wellington	365	Wellington	358	Wellington	357	Wellington	357	Wellington	357	Wellington
366	Newport	366	Newport	359	Newport	358	Newport	358	Newport	358	Newport

1851	1861	1871	1881	1891	1901
Staffordshire					
367 Stafford	367 Stafford	360 Stafford	359 Stafford	359 Stafford	359 Stafford
368 Stone	368 Stone	361 Stone	360 Stone	360 Stone	360 Stone
369 Newcastle under Lyme	369 Newcastle under Lyme	362 Newcastle under Lyme	361 Newcastle under Lyme	361 Newcastle under Lyme	361 Newcastle under Lyme
370 Wolstanton	370 Wolstanton	363 Wolstanton	362 Wolstanton	362 Wolstanton	362 Wolstanton
371 Stoke on Trent	371 Stoke on Trent	364 Stoke on Trent	363 Stoke on Trent	363 Stoke on Trent	363 Stoke on Trent
372 Leek	372 Leek	365 Leek	364 Leek	364 Leek	364 Leek
373 Cheadle	373 Cheadle	366 Cheadle	365 Cheadle	365 Cheadle	365 Cheadle
374 Uttoxeter	374 Uttoxeter	367 Uttoxeter	366 Uttoxeter	366 Uttoxeter	366 Uttoxeter
375 Burton upon Trent	375 Burton upon Trent	368 Burton upon Trent	367 Burton upon Trent	367 Burton upon Trent	367 Burton upon Trent
376 Tamworth	376 Tamworth	369 Tamworth	368 Tamworth	368 Tamworth	368 Tamworth
377 Lichfield	377 Lichfield	370 Lichfield	369 Lichfield	369 Lichfield	369 Lichfield
378 Penkridge	378 Penkridge	371 Penkridge	370 Cannock	370 Cannock	370 Cannock
379 Wolverhampton	379 Wolverhampton	372 Wolverhampton	371 Wolverhampton	371 Wolverhampton	371 Wolverhampton
380 Walsall	380 Walsall	373 Walsall	372 Walsall	372 Walsall	372 Walsall
381 West Bromwich	381 West Bromwich	374 West Bromwich	373 West Bromwich	373 West Bromwich	373 West Bromwich
382 Dudley	382 Dudley	375 Dudley	374 Dudley	374 Dudley	374 Dudley
Worcestershire					
383 Stourbridge	383 Stourbridge	376 Stourbridge	375 Stourbridge	375 Stourbridge	375 Stourbridge
384 Kidderminster	384 Kidderminster	377 Kidderminster	376 Kidderminster	376 Kidderminster	376 Kidderminster
385 Tenbury	385 Tenbury	378 Tenbury	377 Tenbury	377 Tenbury	377 Tenbury
386 Martley	386 Martley	379 Martley	378 Martley	378 Martley	378 Martley
387 Worcester	387 Worcester	380 Worcester	379 Worcester	379 Worcester	379 Worcester
388 Upton on Severn	388 Upton on Severn	381 Upton on Severn	380 Upton on Severn	380 Upton on Severn	380 Upton on Severn
389 Evesham	389 Evesham	382 Evesham	381 Evesham	381 Evesham	381 Evesham
390 Pershore	390 Pershore	383 Pershore	382 Pershore	382 Pershore	382 Pershore
391 Droitwich	391 Droitwich	384 Droitwich	383 Droitwich	383 Droitwich	383 Droitwich
392 Bromsgrove	392 Bromsgrove	385 Bromsgrove	384 Bromsgrove	384 Bromsgrove	384 Bromsgrove
393 King's Norton	393 King's Norton	386 King's Norton	385 King's Norton	385 King's Norton	385 King's Norton
Warwickshire					
394 Birmingham	394 Birmingham	387 Birmingham	386 Birmingham	386 Birmingham	386 Birmingham

	1851	1861	1871	1881	1891	1901
Aston	395	395	388	387	387	387
Meriden	396	396	389	388	388	388
Atherstone	397	397	390	389	389	389
Nuneaton	398	398	391	390	390	390
Foleshill	399	399	392	391	391	391
Coventry	400	400	393	392	392	392
Rugby	401	401	394	393	393	393
Solihull	402	402	395	394	394	394
Warwick	403	403	396	395	395	395
Stratford on Avon	404	404	397	396	396	396
Alcester	405	405	398	397	397	397
Shipston on Stour	406	406	399	398	398	398
Southam	407	407	400	399	399	399
Leicestershire						
Lutterworth	408	408	401	400	400	400
Market Harborough	409	409	402	401	401	401
Billesdon	410	410	403	402	402	402
Blaby	411	411	404	403	403	403
Hinckley	412	412	405	404	404	404
Market Bosworth	413	413	406	405	405	405
Ashby de la Zouch	414	414	407	406	406	406
Loughborough	415	415	408	407	407	407
Barrow on Soar	416	416	409	408	408	408
Leicester	417	417	410	409	409	409
Melton Mowbray	418	418	411	410	410	410
Rutland						
Oakham	419	419	412	411	411	411
Uppingham	420	420	413	412	412	412
Lincolnshire						
Stamford	421	421	414	413	413	413

1851	1861	1871	1881	1891	1901
422 Bourne	422 Bourne	415 Bourne	414 Bourne	414 Bourne	414 Bourne
423 Spalding	423 Spalding	416 Spalding	415 Spalding	415 Spalding	415 Spalding
424 Holbeach	424 Holbeach	417 Holbeach	416 Holbeach	416 Holbeach	416 Holbeach
425 Boston	425 Boston	418 Boston	417 Boston	417 Boston	417 Boston
426 Sleaford	426 Sleaford	419 Sleaford	418 Sleaford	418 Sleaford	418 Sleaford
427 Grantham	427 Grantham	420 Grantham	419 Grantham	419 Grantham	419 Grantham
428 Lincoln	428 Lincoln	421 Lincoln	420 Lincoln	420 Lincoln	420 Lincoln
429 Horncastle	429 Horncastle	422 Horncastle	421 Horncastle	421 Horncastle	421 Horncastle
430 Spilsby	430 Spilsby	423 Spilsby	422 Spilsby	422 Spilsby	422 Spilsby
431 Louth	431 Louth	424 Louth	423 Louth	423 Louth	423 Louth
Little (pt Louth)	Little (pt Louth)	Little (pt Louth)	Little (pt Louth)	Little (pt Louth)	424A Grimsby
Great (pt Caistor)	Great (pt Caistor)	Great (pt Caistor)	Great (pt Caistor)	Great (pt Caistor)	424B Caistor
432 Caistor	432 Caistor	425 Caistor	424 Caistor	424 Caistor	
433 Glanford Brigg	433 Glanford Brigg	426 Glanford Brigg	425 Glanford Brigg	425 Glanford Brigg	425 Glanford Brigg
434 Gainsborough	434 Gainsborough	427 Gainsborough	426 Gainsborough	426 Gainsborough	426 Gainsborough

Nottinghamshire

1851	1861	1871	1881	1891	1901
435 East Retford	435 East Retford	428 East Retford	427 East Retford	427 East Retford	427 East Retford
436 Worksop	436 Worksop	429 Worksop	428 Worksop	428 Worksop	428 Worksop
437 Mansfield	437 Mansfield	430 Mansfield	429 Mansfield	429 Mansfield	429 Mansfield
438 Basford	438 Basford	431 Basford	430 Basford	430 Basford	430 Basford
439 Radford	439 Radford	432 Radford	ptNottingham	ptNottingham	ptNottingham
440 Nottingham	440 Nottingham	433 Nottingham	431 Nottingham	431 Nottingham	431 Nottingham
441 Southwell	441 Southwell	434 Southwell	432 Southwell	432 Southwell	432 Southwell
442 Newark	442 Newark	435 Newark	433 Newark	433 Newark	433 Newark
443 Bingham	443 Bingham	436 Bingham	434 Bingham	434 Bingham	434 Bingham

Derbyshire

1851	1861	1871	1881	1891	1901
444 Shardlow	444 Shardlow	437 Shardlow	435 Shardlow	435 Shardlow	435 Shardlow
445 Derby	445 Derby	438 Derby	436 Derby	436 Derby	436 Derby
446 Belper	446 Belper	439 Belper	437 Belper	437 Belper	437 Belper
447 Ashbourne	447 Ashbourne	440 Ashbourne	438 Ashbourne	438 Ashbourne	438 Ashbourne
448 Chesterfield	448 Chesterfield	441 Chesterfield	439 Chesterfield	439 Chesterfield	439 Chesterfield

1851	1861	1871	1881	1891	1901
449 Bakewell	449 Bakewell	442 Bakewell	440 Bakewell	440 Bakewell	440 Bakewell
450 Chapel en le Frith pt Hayfield	450 Chapel en le Frith pt Hayfield	443 Chapel en le Frith pt Hayfield	441 Chapel en le Frith pt Hayfield	441 Chapel en le Frith pt Hayfield	441 Chapel en le Frith
					442A Glossop
451 Hayfield	451 Hayfield	444 Hayfield	442 Hayfield	442 Hayfield	442B Hayfield

Cheshire

1851	1861	1871	1881	1891	1901
452 Stockport	452 Stockport	445 Stockport	443 Stockport	443 Stockport	443 Stockport
453 Macclesfield	453 Macclesfield	446 Macclesfield	444 Macclesfield	444 Macclesfield	444 Macclesfield
454 Altrincham	454 Altrincham	447 Altrincham	445 Altrincham	445 Altrincham	445 Bucklow
455 Runcorn	455 Runcorn	448 Runcorn	446 Runcorn	446 Runcorn	446 Runcorn
456 Northwich	456 Northwich	449 Northwich	447 Northwich	447 Northwich	447 Northwich
457 Congleton	457 Congleton	450 Congleton	448 Congleton	448 Congleton	448 Congleton
458 Nantwich	458 Nantwich	451 Nantwich	449 Nantwich	449 Nantwich	449 Nantwich
459 Great Boughton	459 Great Boughton	452 Chester	450 Chester	450 Chester	450 Chester
460 Wirral pt Wirral	460A Wirral	453 Wirral	451 Wirral	451 Wirral	451 Wirral
	460B Birkenhead	454 Birkenhead	452 Birkenhead	452 Birkenhead	452 Birkenhead

Lancashire

1851	1861	1871	1881	1891	1901
461 Liverpool pt Liverpool	461 Liverpool pt Liverpool	455 Liverpool pt Liverpool	453 Liverpool	453 Liverpool	453 Liverpool
			454 Toxteth Park	454 Toxteth Park	454 Toxteth Park
462 West Derby	462 West Derby	456 West Derby	455 West Derby	455 West Derby	455 West Derby
463 Prescot	463 Prescot	457 Prescot	456 Prescot	456 Prescot	456 Prescot
464 Ormskirk	464 Ormskirk	458 Ormskirk	457 Ormskirk	457 Ormskirk	457 Ormskirk
465 Wigan	465 Wigan	459 Wigan	458 Wigan	458 Wigan	458 Wigan
466 Warrington	466 Warrington	460 Warrington	459 Warrington	459 Warrington	459 Warrington
467 Leigh	467 Leigh	461 Leigh	460 Leigh	460 Leigh	460 Leigh
468 Bolton	468 Bolton	462 Bolton	461 Bolton	461 Bolton	461 Bolton
469 Bury	469 Bury	463 Bury	462 Bury	462 Bury	462 Bury
470 Barton upon Irwell	470 Barton upon Irwell	464 Barton upon Irwell	463 Barton upon Irwell	463 Barton upon Irwell	463 Barton upon Irwell
471 Chorlton	471 Chorlton	465 Chorlton	464 Chorlton	464 Chorlton	464 Chorlton
472 Salford	472 Salford	466 Salford	465 Salford	465 Salford	465 Salford
473 Manchester pt Manchester	473 Manchester pt Manchester	467 Manchester pt Manchester	466 Manchester	466 Manchester	466 Manchester
			467 Prestwich	467 Prestwich	467 Prestwich

1851	1861	1871	1881	1891	1901
474 Ashton under Lyne	474 Ashton under Lyne	468 Ashton under Lyne	468 Ashton under Lyne	468 Ashton under Lyne	468 Ashton under Lyne
475 Oldham	475 Oldham	469 Oldham	469 Oldham	469 Oldham	469 Oldham
476 Rochdale	476 Rochdale	470 Rochdale	470 Rochdale	470 Rochdale	470 Rochdale
477 Haslingden	477 Haslingden	471 Haslingden	471 Haslingden	471 Haslingden	471 Haslingden
478 Burnley	478 Burnley	472 Burnley	472 Burnley	472 Burnley	472 Burnley
479 Clitheroe	479 Clitheroe	473 Clitheroe	473 Clitheroe	473 Clitheroe	473 Clitheroe
480 Blackburn	480 Blackburn	474 Blackburn	474 Blackburn	474 Blackburn	474 Blackburn
481 Chorley	481 Chorley	475 Chorley	475 Chorley	475 Chorley	475 Chorley
482 Preston	482 Preston	476 Preston	476 Preston	476 Preston	476 Preston.
483 Fylde	483 Fylde	477 Fylde	477 Fylde	477 Fylde	477 Fylde
484 Garstang	484 Garstang	478 Garstang	478 Garstang	478 Garstang	478 Garstang
485 Lancaster	485 Lancaster	479 Lancaster	479 Lancaster	479 Lancaster	479 Lancaster
pt Lancaster		480 Lunesdale	480 Lunesdale	480 Lunesdale	480 Lunesdale
486 Ulverston	486 Ulverston	481 Ulverston	481 Ulverston	481 Ulverston	481 Ulverston
pt Ulverston	pt Ulverston	pt Ulverston	482 Barrow in Furness	482 Barrow in Furness	482 Barrow in Furness
W. Riding Yorkshire					
487 Sedbergh	487 Sedbergh	482 Sedbergh	483 Sedburgh	483 Sedbergh	483 Sedbergh
488 Settle	488 Settle	483 Settle	484 Settle	484 Settle	484 Settle
489 Skipton	489 Skipton	484 Skipton	485 Skipton	485 Skipton	485 Skipton
490 Pateley Bridge	490 Pateley Bridge	485 Pateley Bridge	486 Pateley Bridge	486 Pateley Bridge	486 Pateley Bridge
491 Ripon	491 Ripon	486 Ripon	487 Ripon	487 Ripon	487 Ripon
pt Knaresborough	492A Great Ouseburn	487 Great Ouseburn	488 Great Ouseburn	488 Great Ouseburn	488 Great Ouseburn
492 Knaresborough	492B Knaresborough	488 Knaresborough	489 Knaresborough	489 Knaresborough	489 Knaresborough
pt Knaresborough	492C Wetherby	489 Wetherby	490 Wetherby	490 Wetherby	490 Wetherby
pt Knaresborough	492D Kirk Deighton	pt Wetherby	pt Wetherby	pt Wetherby	pt Wetherby
		pt Wharfedale	pt Wharfedale	pt Wharfedale	pt Wharfedale
493 Otley	493A Otley				
pt Otley					
493B Wharfedale	493B Wharfedale	490 Wharfedale	491 Wharfedale	491 Wharfedale	491 Wharfedale
494 Keighley	494 Keighley	491 Keighley	492 Keighley	492 Keighley	492 Keighley
495 Todmorden	495 Todmorden	492 Todmorden	493 Todmorden	493 Todmorden	493 Todmorden
496 Saddleworth	496 Saddleworth	493 Saddleworth	494 Saddleworth	494 Saddleworth	494 Saddleworth
497 Huddersfield	497 Huddersfield	494 Huddersfield	495 Huddersfield	495 Huddersfield	495 Huddersfield

1851		1861		1871		1881		1891		1901	
498	Halifax	498	Halifax	495	Halifax	496	Halifax	496	Halifax	496	Halifax
499	Bradford	499	Bradford	496	Bradford	497	Bradford	497	Bradford	497A	Bradford
	pt Pontefract		pt Bradford		pt Bradford		pt Bradford		pt Bradford	497B	North Bierley
500	Hunslet	500	Hunslet	497	Hunslet	498	Hunslet	498	Hunslet	498	Hunslet
	pt Hunslet		pt Hunslet	498	Holbeck	499	Holbeck	499	Holbeck	499	Holbeck
	pt Hunslet		pt Hunslet	499	Bramley	500	Bramley	500	Bramley	500	Bramley
501	Leeds	501	Leeds	500	Leeds	501	Leeds	501	Leeds	501	Leeds
502	Dewsbury	502	Dewsbury	501	Dewsbury	502	Dewsbury	502	Dewsbury	502	Dewsbury
503	Wakefield	503	Wakefield	502	Wakefield	503	Wakefield	503	Wakefield	503	Wakefield
504	Pontefract	504A	Pontefract	503	Pontefract	504	Pontefract	504	Pontefract	504	Pontefract
	pt Pontefract	504B	Hemsworth	504	Hemsworth	505	Hemsworth	505	Hemsworth	505	Hemsworth
505	Barnsley	505	Barnsley	505	Barnsley	506	Barnsley	506	Barnsley	506	Barnsley
506	Wortley	506	Wortley	506	Wortley	507	Wortley	507	Wortley	507	Wortley
507	Ecclesall Bierlow	507	Ecclesall Bierlow	507	Ecclesall Bierlow	508	Ecclesall Bierlow	508	Ecclesall Bierlow	508	Ecclesall Bierlow
508	Sheffield	508	Sheffield	508	Sheffield	509	Sheffield	509	Sheffield	509	Sheffield
509	Rotherham	509	Rotherham	509	Rotherham	510	Rotherham	510	Rotherham	510	Rotherham
510	Doncaster	510	Doncaster	510	Doncaster	511	Doncaster	511	Doncaster	511	Doncaster
511	Thorne	511	Thorne	511	Thorne	512	Thorne	512	Thorne	512	Thorne
512	Goole	512	Goole	512	Goole	513	Goole	513	Goole	513	Goole
513	Selby	513	Selby	513	Selby	514	Selby	514	Selby	514	Selby
514	Tadcaster	514	Tadcaster	514	Tadcaster	515	Tadcaster	515	Tadcaster	515	Tadcaster

E. Riding Yorkshire

1851		1861		1871		1881		1891		1901	
515	York	515	York	515	York	516	York	516	York	516	York
516	Pocklington	516	Pocklington	516	Pocklington	517	Pocklington	517	Pocklington	517	Pocklington
517	Howden	517	Howden	517	Howden	518	Howden	518	Howden	518	Howden
518	Beverley	518	Beverley	518	Beverley	519	Beverley	519	Beverley	519	Beverley
519	Sculcoates	519	Sculcoates	519	Sculcoates	520	Sculcoates	520	Sculcoates	520	Sculcoates
520	Hull	520	Hull	520	Hull	521	Hull	521	Hull	521	Hull
521	Patrington	521	Patrington	521	Patrington	522	Patrington	522	Patrington	522	Patrington
522	Skirlaugh	522	Skirlaugh	522	Skirlaugh	523	Skirlaugh	523	Skirlaugh	523	Skirlaugh
523	Driffield	523	Driffield	523	Driffield	524	Driffield	524	Driffield	524	Driffield

1851		1861		1871		1881		1891		1901	
524	Bridlington	524	Bridlington	524	Bridlington	525	Bridlington	525	Bridlington	525	Bridlington

N. Riding Yorkshire

1851		1861		1871		1881		1891		1901	
525	Scarborough	525	Scarborough	525	Scarborough	526	Scarborough	526	Scarborough	526	Scarborough
526	Malton	526	Malton	526	Malton	527	Malton	527	Malton	527	Malton
527	Easingwold	527	Easingwold	527	Easingwold	528	Easingwold	528	Easingwold	528	Easingwold
528	Thirsk	528	Thirsk	528	Thirsk	529	Thirsk	529	Thirsk	529	Thirsk
529	Helmsley	529	Helmsley	529	Helmsley	530	Helmsley	530	Helmsley	530	Helmsley
530	Pickering	530	Pickering	530	Pickering	531	Pickering	531	Pickering	531	Pickering
531	Whitby	531	Whitby	531	Whitby	532	Whitby	532	Whitby	532	Whitby
532	Guisborough	532	Guisborough	532	Guisborough	533	Guisborough	533	Guisborough	533	Guisborough
	pt Guisborough		pt Guisborough		pt Guisborough						
						534	Middlesbrough	534	Middlesbrough	534	Middlesbrough
533	Stokesley	533	Stokesley	533	Stokesley	535	Stokesley	535	Stokesley	535	Stokesley
534	Northallerton	534	Northallerton	534	Northallerton	536	Northallerton	536	Northallerton	536	Northallerton
535	Bedale	535	Bedale	535	Bedale	537	Bedale	537	Bedale	537	Bedale
536	Leyburn	536	Leyburn	536	Leyburn	538	Leyburn	538	Leyburn	538	Leyburn
537	Askrigg	537	Askrigg	537	Aysgarth	539	Aysgarth	539	Aysgarth	539	Aysgarth
538	Reeth	538	Reeth	538	Reeth	540	Reeth	540	Reeth	540	Reeth
539	Richmond	539	Richmond	539	Richmond	541	Richmond	541	Richmond	541	Richmond

Durham

1851		1861		1871		1881		1891		1901	
540	Darlington	540	Darlington	540	Darlington	542	Darlington	542	Darlington	542	Darlington
541	Stockton	541A	Stockton	541	Stockton	543	Stockton	543	Stockton	543A	Stockton
	pt Stockton		pt Stockton		pt Stockton		pt Stockton		pt Stockton	543B	Sedgefield
	pt Stockton	541B	Hartlepool	542	Hartlepool	544	Hartlepool	544	Hartlepool	544	Hartlepool
542	Auckland	542	Auckland	543	Auckland	545	Auckland	545	Auckland	545	Auckland
543	Teesdale	543	Teesdale	544	Teesdale	546	Teesdale	546	Teesdale	546	Teesdale
544	Weardale	544	Weardale	545	Weardale	547	Weardale	547	Weardale	547	Weardale
	pt Weardale		pt Weardale		pt Weardale	548	Lanchester	548	Lanchester	548	Lanchester
545	Durham	545	Durham	546	Durham	549	Durham	549	Durham	549	Durham
546	Easington	546	Easington	547	Easington	550	Easington	550	Easington	550	Easington
547	Houghton le Spring	547	Houghton le Spring	548	Houghton le Spring	551	Houghton le Spring	551	Houghton le Spring	551	Houghton le Spring
548	Chester le Street	548	Chester le Street	549	Chester le Street	552	Chester le Street	552	Chester le Street	552	Chester le Street

District	1851	1861	1871	1881	1891	1901
Sunderland	549	549	550	553	553	553
South Shields	550	550	551	554	554	554
Gateshead	551	551	552	555	555	555
Northumberland						
Newcastle upon Tyne	552	552	553	556	556	556
Tynemouth	553	553	554	557	557	557
Castle Ward	554	554	555	558	558	558
Hexham	555	555	556	559	559	559
Haltwhistle	556	556	557	560	560	560
Bellingham	557	557	558	561	561	561
Morpeth	558	558	559	562	562	562
Alnwick	559	559	560	563	563	563
Belford	560	560	561	564	564	564
Berwick	561	561	562	565	565	565
Glendale	562	562	563	566	566	566
Rothbury	563	563	564	567	567	567
Cumberland						
Alston	564	564	565	568	568	568
Penrith	565	565	566	569	569	569
Brampton	566	566	567	570	570	570
Longtown	567	567	568	571	571	571
Carlisle	568	568	569	572	572	572
Wigton	569	569	570	573	573	573
Cockermouth	570	570	571	574	574	574
Whitehaven	571	571	572	575	575	575
Bootle	572	572	573	576	576	576
Westmoreland						
East Ward	573	573	574	577	577	577
West Ward	574	574	575	578	578	578
Kendal	575	575	576	579	579	579
Monmouthshire						
Chepstow	576	576	577	580	580	580

1851		1861		1871		1881		1891		1901	
577	Monmouth	577	Monmouth	578	Monmouth	581	Monmouth	581	Monmouth	581	Monmouth
578	Abergavenny	578A	Abergavenny	579	Abergavenny	582	Abergavenny	582	Abergavenny	582	Abergavenny
	pt Abergavenny	578B	Bedwellty	580	Bedwellty	583	Bedwellty	583	Bedwellty	583	Bedwellty
579	Pontypool	579	Pontypool	581	Pontypool	584	Pontypool	584	Pontypool	584	Pontypool
580	Newport	580	Newport	582	Newport	585	Newport	585	Newport	585	Newport
Glamorgan											
581	Cardiff	581	Cardiff	583	Cardiff	586	Cardiff	586	Cardiff	586	Cardiff
	pt Cardiff		pt Cardiff	584	Pontypridd	587	Pontypridd	587	Pontypridd	587	Pontypridd
582	Merthyr Tydfil	582	Merthyr Tydfil	585	Merthyr Tydfil	588	Merthyr Tydfil	588	Merthyr Tydfil	588	Merthyr Tydfil
583	Bridgend	583	Bridgend	586	Bridgend	589	Bridgend	589	Bridgend	589	Bridgend
584	Neath	584	Neath	587	Neath	590	Neath	590	Neath	590	Neath
	pt Neath		pt Neath		pt Neath	591	Pontardawe	591	Pontardawe	591	Pontardawe
585	Swansea	585A	Swansea	588	Swansea	592	Swansea	592	Swansea	592	Swansea
	pt Swansea	585B	Gower	589	Gower	593	Gower	593	Gower	593	Gower
Carmarthen											
586	Llanelly	586	Llanelly	590	Llanelly	594	Llanelly	594	Llanelly	594	Llanelly
587	Llandovery	587	Llandovery	591	Llandovery	595	Llandovery	595	Llandovery	595	Llandovery
588	Llandilofawr	588	Llandilofawr	592	Llandilofawr	596	Llandilofawr	596	Llandilofawr	596	Llandilofawr
589	Carmarthen	589	Carmarthen	593	Carmarthen	597	Carmarthen	597	Carmarthen	597	Carmarthen
Pembroke											
590	Narberth	590	Narberth	594	Narberth	598	Narberth	598	Narberth	598	Narberth
591	Pembroke	591	Pembroke	595	Pembroke	599	Pembroke	599	Pembroke	599	Pembroke
592	Haverfordwest	592	Haverfordwest	596	Haverfordwest	600	Haverfordwest	600	Haverfordwest	600	Haverfordwest
Cardiganshire											
593	Cardigan	593	Cardigan	597	Cardigan	601	Cardigan	601	Cardigan	601	Cardigan
594	Newcastle in Emlyn	594	Newcastle in Emlyn	598	Newcastle in Emlyn	602	Newcastle in Emlyn	602	Newcastle in Emlyn	602	Newcastle in Emlyn
595	Lampeter	595	Lampeter	599	Lampeter	603	Lampeter	603	Lampeter	603	Lampeter
596	Aberayron	596	Aberayron	600	Aberayron	604	Aberayron	604	Aberayron	604	Aberayron
597	Aberystwyth	597	Aberystwyth	601	Aberystwyth	605	Aberystwyth	605	Aberystwyth	605	Aberystwyth
598	Tregaron	598	Tregaron	602	Tregaron	606	Tregaron	606	Tregaron	606	Tregaron
Brecon											
599	Builth	599	Builth	603	Builth	607	Builth	607	Builth	607	Builth

1851	1861	1871	1881	1891	1901
600 Brecknock	600 Brecknock	604 Brecknock	608 Brecknock	608 Brecknock	608 Brecknock
601 Crickhowell	601 Crickhowell	605 Crickhowell	609 Crickhowell	609 Crickhowell	609 Crickhowell
602 Hay	602 Hay	606 Hay	610 Hay	610 Hay	610 Hay
Radnorshire					
603 Presteigne	603 Presteigne	607 Presteigne	pt Knighton	pt Knighton	pt Knighton
604 Knighton	604 Knighton	608 Knighton	611 Knighton	611 Knighton	611 Knighton
605 Rhayader	605 Rhayader	609 Rhayader	612 Rhayader	612 Rhayader	612 Rhayader
Montgomery					
606 Machynlleth	606 Machynlleth	610 Machynlleth	613 Machynlleth	613 Machynlleth	613 Machynlleth
607 Newtown	607 Newtown	611 Newtown	614 Newtown	614 Newtown	614 Newtown
608 Montgomery	608 Montgomery	612 Forden	615 Forden	615 Forden	615 Forden
609 Llanfyllin	609 Llanfyllin	613 Llanfyllin	616 Llanfyllin	616 Llanfyllin	616 Llanfyllin
Flintshire					
610 Holywell	610 Holywell	614 Holywell	617 Holywell	617 Holywell	617 Holywell
Denbighshire					
611 Wrexham	611 Wrexham	615 Wrexham	618 Wrexham	618 Wrexham	618 Wrexham
612 Ruthin	612 Ruthin	616 Ruthin	619 Ruthin	619 Ruthin	619 Ruthin
613 St Asaph	613 St Asaph	617 St Asaph	620 St Asaph	620 St Asaph	620 St Asaph
614 Llanrwst	614 Llanrwst	618 Llanrwst	621 Llanrwst	621 Llanrwst	621 Llanrwst
Merioneth					
615 Corwen	615 Corwen	619 Corwen	622 Corwen	622 Corwen	622 Corwen
616 Bala	616 Bala	620 Bala	623 Bala	623 Bala	623 Bala
617 Dolgellau	617 Dolgellau	621 Dolgellau	624 Dolgellau	624 Dolgellau	624 Dolgellau
618 Ffestiniog	618 Ffestiniog	622 Ffestiniog	625 Ffestiniog	625 Ffestiniog	625 Ffestiniog
Caernarfon					
619 Pwllheli	619 Pwllheli	623 Pwllheli	626 Pwllheli	626 Pwllheli	626 Pwllheli
620 Caernarfon	620 Caernarfon	624 Caernarfon	627 Caernarfon	627 Caernarfon	627 Caernarfon
621 Bangor	621 Bangor	625 Bangor	628 Bangor	628 Bangor	628 Bangor
622 Conway	622 Conway	626 Conway	629 Conway	629 Conway	629 Conway
Anglesey					
623 Anglesey pt Anglesey	623 Anglesey pt Anglesey	627 Anglesey pt Anglesey	630 Anglesey pt Anglesey	630 Anglesey	630 Anglesey
				631 Holyhead	631 Holyhead

Appendix 8: Street indexes 1841

All London registration districts

RD no.	Place	RD no.	Place
474	Ashton under Lyne	582	Merthyr Tydfil
394	Aston	552	Newcastle upon Tyne
470	Barton upon Irwell	553	North Shields
329	Bedminster	234	Norwich
394	Birmingham	440	Nottingham
474	Bolton	475	Oldham
499	Bradford	96	Portsmouth
329	Bristol	452	Prestbury
469	Bury	475	Prestwich
471	Chorlton	476	Rochdale
46	Croydon	471	Salford
382	Dudley	520	Sculcoates
508	Ecclesall Bierlow	508	Sheffield
550	Gateshead	105	Southampton
498	Halifax	550	South Shields
497	Huddersfield	105	South Stoneham
520	Hull	549	Sunderland
501	Leeds	462	Toxteth Park
461	Liverpool	553	Tynemouth
452	Macclesfield	462	West Derby
472	Manchester Town		

Appendix 9: Street indexes 1851

All London registration districts

RD no.	Place	RD no.	Place	RD no.	Place
46	Croydon	360	Shrewsbury	481	Chorley
47	Kingston	365	Wellington	482	Preston
54	Medway	367	Stafford	485	Lancaster
57	Tonbridge	371	Stoke on Trent	495	Todmorden
58	Maidstone	379	Wolverhampton	496	Saddleworth
85	Brighton	380	Walsall	497	Huddersfield
92	Chichester	381	West Bromwich	498	Halifax
96	Portsea	382	Dudley	499	Bradford
99	Isle of Wight	383	Stourbridge	500	Hunslet
105	Southampton	384	Kidderminster	501	Leeds
106	South Stoneham	387	Worcester	502	Dewsbury
127	Reading	393	King's Norton	503	Wakefield
134	Brentford	394	Birmingham	506	Wortley
135	Hendon	395	Aston	507	Ecclesall Bierlow
136	Barnet	400	Coventry	508	Sheffield
137	Edmonton	417	Leicester	509	Rotherham
158	Oxford	421	Stamford	515	York
168	Northampton	424	Holbeach	519	Sculcoates
179	Bedford	428	Lincoln	520	Hull
183	Leighton Buzzard	440	Nottingham	531	Whitby
184	Luton	445	Derby	541	Stockton
187	Cambridge	452	Stockport	545	Durham
194	West Ham	453	Macclesfield	549	Sunderland
215	Bury St Edmunds	459	Chester	550	South Shields
222	Ipswich	460A	Wirral	551	Gateshead
228	Yarmouth	460B	Birkenhead	552	Newcastle upon Tyne
234	Norwich	461	Liverpool		
246	King's Lynn	462	West Derby	553	Tynemouth
264	Salisbury	463	Prescot	568	Carlisle
281	St Thomas	465	Wigan	570	Cockermouth
282	Exeter	466	Warrington	578	Abergavenny
287	Plymouth	468	Bolton	580	Newport
288	East Stonehouse	469	Bury	581	Cardiff
289	Stoke Damerel	470	Barton upon Irwerl	582	Merthyr Tydfil
316	Bridgwater	471	Chorlton	583	Bridgend
326	Bath	472	Salford	584	Neath
327	Keynsham	473	Manchester	585	Swansea
328	Bedminster	474	Ashton under Lyne	598	Tregaron
329	Bristol	475	Oldham	620	Caernarfon
330	Clifton	476	Rochdale	800	Isle of Man
336	Gloucester	477	Haslingden	900	Jersey
344	Cheltenham	480	Blackburn		

William Hill, Bookkeeper (HO 107/2202, f. 8, p. 8)

Appendix 10: Street indexes 1861 and 1871

All London registration districts

1861		1871	
RD no.	Place	RD no.	Place
46	Croydon	37	Croydon
47	Kingston	38	Kingston
54	Medway	45	Medway
57	Tonbridge	48	Tonbridge
58	Maidstone	49	Maidstone
85	Brighton	76	Brighton
96	Portsea	87	Portsea
105	Southampton	96	Southampton
106	South Stoneham	97	South Stoneham
127	Reading	118	Reading
134	Brentford	125	Brentford
135	Hendon	126	Hendon
137	Edmonton	128	Edmonton
158	Oxford	149	Oxford
168	Northampton	159	Northampton
187	Cambridge	178	Cambridge
194	West Ham	185	West Ham
222	Ipswich	213	Ipswich
228	Yarmouth	219	Yarmouth
234	Norwich	225	Norwich
282	Exeter	272	Exeter
287	Plymouth	277	Plymouth
288	East Stonehouse	278	East Stonehouse
289	Stoke Damerel	279	Stoke Damerel
326	Bath	317	Bath
327	Keynsham	318	Keynsham
328	Bedminster	319	Bedminster
329	Bristol	320	Bristol
330	Clifton	321	Clifton
336	Gloucester	327	Gloucester
344	Cheltenham	335	Cheltenham
371	Stoke on Trent	364	Stoke on Trent
379	Wolverhampton	372	Wolverhampton
381	West Bromwich	374	West Bromwich
382	Dudley	375	Dudley
383	Stourbridge	376	Stourbridge
387	Worcester	380	Worcester
393	King's Norton	386	King's Norton
394	Birmingham	387	Birmingham
395	Aston	388	Aston
400	Coventry	393	Coventry
417	Leicester	410	Leicester

Thomas R Ravenscroft, Army Tailor (RG 11/1182, f. 67, p. 23)

1861		1871	
RD no.	Place	RD no.	Place
440	Nottingham	433	Nottingham
445	Derby	438	Derby
452	Stockport	445	Stockport
453	Macclesfield	446	Macclesfield
459	Chester	452	Chester
460A	Wirral	453	Wirral
460B	Birkenhead	454	Birkenhead
461	Liverpool	455	Liverpool
462	West Derby	456	West Derby
465	Wigan	459	Wigan
468	Bolton	462	Bolton
469	Bury	463	Bury
470	Barton upon Irwell	464	Barton upon Irwell
471	Chorlton	465	Chorlton
472	Salford	466	Salford
473	Manchester	467	Manchester
474	Ashton under Lyne	468	Ashton under Lyne
475	Oldham	469	Oldham
476	Rochdale	470	Rochdale
477	Haslingden	471	Haslingden
480	Blackburn	474	Blackburn
481	Chorley	475	Chorley
482	Preston	476	Preston
485	Lancaster	479	Lancaster
495	Todmorden	492	Todmorden
496	Saddleworth	493	Saddleworth
497	Huddersfield	494	Huddersfield
498	Halifax	495	Halifax
499	Bradford	496	Bradford
500	Hunslet	597	Hunslet
	pt Hunslet	498	Holbeck
	pt Hunslet	499	Bramley
501	Leeds	500	Leeds
506	Wortley	506	Wortley
507	Ecclesall Bierlow	507	Ecclesall Bierlow
508	Sheffield	508	Sheffield
509	Rotherham	509	Rotherham
515	York	515	York
519	Sculcoates	519	Sculcoates
520	Hull	520	Hull
541A	Stockton	541	Stockton
549	Sunderland	550	Sunderland

Arnold Dolnetch, Teacher of Music (RG 12 / 461, f. 116, p. 41)

1861		1871	
RD no.	**Place**	**RD no.**	**Place**
550	South Shields	551	South Shields
551	Gateshead	552	Gateshead
552	Newcastle upon Tyne	553	Newcastle upon Tyne
553	Tynemouth	554	Tynemouth
568	Carlisle	569	Carlisle
580	Newport	582	Newport
581	Cardiff	583	Cardiff
582	Merthyr Tydfil	585	Merthyr Tydfil
585A	Swansea	588	Swansea
620	Caernarfon	900	Jersey
900	Jersey		

Richard Pilkington, Glass Mftr (RG 12/3027, f. 58, p. 4)

Appendix 11: Street indexes 1881 and 1891

All London registration districts

1881		1891	
RD no.	Place	RD no.	Place
30	Epsom	30	Epsom
32	Guildford	32	Guildford
33	Farnham	33	Farnham
38	Croydon	38	Croydon
39	Kingston	39	Kingston
40	Richmond	40	Richmond
41	Bromley	41	Bromley
42	Dartford	42	Dartford
46	Medway	46	Medway
49	Tonbridge	49	Tonbridge
50	Maidstone	50	Maidstone
62	Thanet	62	Thanet
64	Dover	64	Dover
65	Elham	65	Elham
68	Hastings	68	Hastings
70	Eastbourne	70	Eastbourne
77	Brighton	77	Brighton
78	Steyning	78	Steyning
88	Portsea	88	Portsea
91	Isle of Wight	91	Isle of Wight
93	Christchurch	93	Christchurch
97	Southampton	97	Southampton
98	South Stoneham	98	South Stoneham
119	Reading	119	Reading
126	Brentford	126	Brentford
127	Hendon	127	Hendon
128	Barnet	128	Barnet
129	Edmonton	129	Edmonton
142	Wycombe	142	Wycombe
149	Headington	149	Headington
150	Oxford	150	Oxford
160	Northampton	160	Northampton
163	Wellingborough	163	Wellingborough
167	Peterborough	167	Peterborough
171	Bedford	171	Bedford
176	Luton	176	Luton
179	Cambridge	179	Cambridge
186	West Ham	186	West Ham
189	Romford	189	Romford
213	Ipswich	213	Ipswich
219	Yarmouth	219	Yarmouth
225	Norwich	225	Norwich

Heathfield H Stephenson, Professional Cricketer (RG 9 / 457, f. 70)

1881		1891	
RD no.	**Place**	**RD no.**	**Place**
241	Highworth	241	Highworth
271	St Thomas	271	St Thomas
272	Exeter	272	Exeter
273	Newton Abbot	273	Newton Abbot
274	Totnes	274	Totnes
277	Plymouth	277	Plymouth
278	East Stonehouse	278	East Stonehouse
279	Stoke Damerel	279	Stoke Damerel
285	Barnstaple	285	Barnstaple
300	Redruth	300	Redruth
301	Penzance	301	Penzance
315	Axbridge	315	Axbridge
317	Bath	317	Bath
318	Keynsham	318	Keynsham
319	Bedminster	319	Bedminster
320	Bristol	320	Bristol
321	Barton Regis	321	Barton Regis
327	Gloucester	327	Gloucester
329	Stroud	329	Stroud
335	Cheltenham	335	Cheltenham
339	Hereford	339	Hereford
351	Atcham	351	Atcham
362	Wolstanton	362	Wolstanton
363	Stoke on Trent	363	Stoke on Trent
367	Burton upon Trent	367	Burton upon Trent
369	Lichfield	369	Lichfield
370	Cannock	370	Cannock
371	Wolverhampton	371	Wolverhampton
372	Walsall	372	Walsall
373	West Bromwich	373	West Bromwich
374	Dudley	374	Dudley
375	Stourbridge	375	Stourbridge
376	Kidderminster	376	Kidderminster
379	Worcester	379	Worcester
385	King's Norton	385	King's Norton
386	Birmingham	386	Birmingham
387	Aston	387	Aston
392	Coventry	392	Coventry
395	Warwick	395	Warwick
409	Leicester	409	Leicester
420	Lincoln	420	Lincoln
424	Caistor	424	Caistor

George Macaulay Trevelyan, scholar (RG 12 / 766, f. 153)

1881		1891	
RD no.	**Place**	**RD no.**	**Place**
425	Glanford Brigg	425	Glanford Brigg
429	Mansfield	429	Mansfield
430	Basford	430	Basford
431	Nottingham	431	Nottingham
435	Shardlow	435	Shardlow
436	Derby	436	Derby
437	Belper	437	Belper
439	Chesterfield	439	Chesterfield
443	Stockport	443	Stockport
444	Macclesfield	444	Macclesfield
445	Altrincham	445	Altrincham
446	Runcorn	446	Runcorn
447	Northwich	447	Northwich
449	Nantwich	449	Nantwich
450	Chester	450	Chester
451	Wirral	451	Wirral
452	Birkenhead	452	Birkenhead
453	Liverpool	453	Liverpool
454	Toxteth Park	454	Toxteth Park
455	West Derby	455	West Derby
456	Prescott	456	Prescott
457	Ormskirk	457	Ormskirk
458	Wigan	458	Wigan
459	Warrington	459	Warrington
460	Leigh	460	Leigh
461	Bolton	461	Bolton
462	Bury	462	Bury
463	Barton upon Irwell	463	Barton upon Irwell
464	Chorlton	464	Chorlton
465	Salford	465	Salford
466	Manchester	466	Manchester
467	Prestwich	467	Prestwich
468	Ashton under Lyne	468	Ashton under Lyne
469	Oldham	469	Oldham
470	Rochdale	470	Rochdale
471	Haslingden	471	Haslingden
472	Burnley	472	Burnley
474	Blackburn	474	Blackburn
475	Chorley	475	Chorley
476	Preston	476	Preston
477	Fylde	477	Fylde
479	Lancaster	479	Lancaster

Alfred Snellgrove, Licensed Victualler, formerly Linen Draper (RG 12 / 323, f. 13, p. 21)

1881		1891	
RD no.	**Place**	**RD no.**	**Place**
481	Ulverston	481	Ulverston
482	Barrow in Furness	482	Barrow in Furness
491	Wharfedale	491	Wharfedale
492	Keighley	492	Keighley
493	Todmorden	493	Todmorden
494	Saddleworth	494	Saddleworth
495	Huddersfield	495	Huddersfield
496	Halifax	496	Halifax
497	Bradford	497	Bradford
498	Hunslet	498	Hunslet
499	Holbeck	499	Holbeck
500	Bramley	500	Bramley
501	Leeds	501	Leeds
502	Dewsbury	502	Dewsbury
503	Wakefield	503	Wakefield
504	Pontefract	504	Pontefract
506	Barnsley	506	Barnsley
507	Wortley	507	Wortley
508	Ecclesall Bierlow	508	Ecclesall Bierlow
509	Sheffield	509	Sheffield
510	Rotherham	510	Rotherham
511	Doncaster	511	Doncaster
516	York	516	York
520	Sculcoates	520	Sculcoates
521	Hull	521	Hull
526	Scarborough	526	Scarborough
533	Guisborough	533	Guisborough
534	Middlesbrough	534	Middlesbrough
542	Darlington	542	Darlington
543	Stockton	543	Stockton
544	Hartlepool	544	Hartlepool
545	Auckland	545	Auckland
548	Lanchester	548	Lanchester
549	Durham	549	Durham
550	Easington	550	Easington
552	Chester le Street	552	Chester le Street
553	Sunderland	553	Sunderland
554	South Shields	554	South Shields
555	Gateshead	555	Gateshead
556	Newcastle upon Tyne	556	Newcastle upon Tyne
557	Tynemouth	557	Tynemouth
562	Morpeth	562	Morpeth

John Dewhurst, Worsted Spinner (RG 10/4403, f. 91)

1881		1891	
RD no.	**Place**	**RD no.**	**Place**
572	Carlisle	572	Carlisle
574	Cockermouth	574	Cockermouth
575	Whitehaven	575	Whitehaven
579	Kendal	579	Kendal
583	Bedwellty	583	Bedwellty
584	Pontypool	584	Pontypool
585	Newport	585	Newport
586	Cardiff	586	Cardiff
587	Pontypridd	587	Pontypridd
588	Merthyr Tydfil	588	Merthyr Tydfil
589	Bridgend	589	Bridgend
590	Neath	590	Neath
592	Swansea	592	Swansea
594	Llanelly	594	Llanelly
617	Holywell	617	Holywell
618	Wrexham	618	Wrexham
627	Caernarfon	627	Caernarfon
900	Jersey	900	Jersey

George Bernard Shaw, Dramatist (RG 11 / 185, f. 35, p. 1)

Appendix 12: Street indexes 1901

All London registration districts

RD no.	Place	RD no.	Place
30	Epsom	193	Rochford
31	Chertsey	195	Tendring
32	Guildford	218	Mutford
33	Farnham	219	Yarmouth
36	Reigate	225	Norwich
38	Croydon	241	Swindon
39	Kingston	264	Weymouth
40	Richmond	271	St Thomas
41	Bromley	273	Newton Abbot
42	Dartford	274	Totnes
44	Stroud	277	Plymouth
46	Medway	279	Devonport
49	Tonbridge	285	Barnstaple
50	Maidstone	300	Redruth
62	Thanet	301	Penzance
64	Dover	315	Axbridge
65	Elham	317	Bath
68	Hastings	320	Bristol
70	Eastbourne	327	Gloucester
77	Brighton	335	Cheltenham
78	Steyning	339	Hereford
88	Portsmouth	351	Atcham
91	Isle of Wight	361	Newcastle under Lyme
93	Christchurch	362	Wolstanton
97	Southampton	363	Stoke on Trent
98	South Stoneham	364	Leek
119	Reading	367	Burton upon Trent
123	Windsor	369	Lichfield
126	Brentford	370	Cannock
127	Hendon	371	Wolverhampton
128	Barnet	372	Walsall
129	Edmonton	373	West Bromwich
137	Watford	374	Dudley
142	Wycombe	375	Stourbridge
160	Northampton	376	Kidderminster
163	Wellingborough	379	Worcester
164	Kettering	385	King's Norton
167	Peterborough	386	Birmingham
171	Bedford	387	Aston
176	Luton	392	Coventry
186	West Ham	394	Solihull
189	Romford	395	Warwick

Annie Besant, Political Author (RG 1 1 1 172, f. 69, p. 39)

RD no.	Place	RD no.	Place
406	Ashby de la Zouch	476	Preston
409	Leicester	477	Fylde
420	Lincoln	479	Lancaster
424A	Grimsby	480	Lunesdale
425	Glanford Brigg	481	Ulverston
429	Mansfield	482	Barrow in Furness
430	Basford	485	Skipton
431	Nottingham	489	Knaresborough
435	Shardlow	491	Wharfedale
436	Derby	492	Keighley
437	Belper	493	Todmorden
439	Chesterfield	495	Huddersfield
443	Stockport	496	Halifax
444	Macclesfield	497A	Bradford
445	Bucklow	498	Hunslet
447	Northwich	500	Bramley
449	Nantwich	501	Leeds
450	Chester	502	Dewsbury
451	Wirral	503	Wakefield
452	Birkenhead	504	Pontefract
453	Liverpool	506	Barnsley
454	Toxteth Park	507	Wortley
455	West Derby	508	Ecclesall Bierlow
456	Prescott	509	Sheffield
457	Ormskirk	510	Rotherham
458	Wigan	511	Doncaster
459	Warrington	516	York
460	Leigh	520	Sculcoates
461	Bolton	521	Hull
462	Bury	526	Scarborough
463	Barton upon Irwell	533	Guisborough
464	Chorlton	534	Middlesbrough
465	Salford	542	Darlington
466	Manchester	543	Stockton
467	Prestwich	544	Hartlepool
468	Ashton under Lyne	545	Auckland
469	Oldham	548	Lanchester
470	Rochdale	550	Easington
471	Haslingden	551	Houghton le Spring
472	Burnley	552	Chester le Street
474	Blackburn	553	Sunderland
475	Chorley	554	South Shields

Frances M Buss, School Mistress [founder of first girls' public school] (RG 11 / 175, f. 96, p. 15)

RD no.	Place	RD no.	Place
555	Gateshead	588	Merthyr Tydfil
556	Newcastle upon Tyne	589	Bridgend
557	Tynemouth	590	Neath
562	Morpeth	592	Swansea
572	Carlisle	594	Llanelly
574	Cockermouth	594	Llanelly
575	Whitehaven	617	Holywell
579	Kendal	617	Holywell
583	Bedwellty	618	Wrexham
585	Newport	618	Wrexham
586	Cardiff	627	Caernarfon
587	Pontypridd	627	Caernarfon

The Duke of Fife and Princess Royal, Mortlake (RG 12/623, f. 155, p. 3)

Appendix 13: Places street-indexed in part

Donated to the census room by various individual indexers

1841	1851	1861	1871	1881
Barnet	Bedford	Barnet	Barnet	Ashby de la Zouch
Barton upon Irwell	Biggleswade	Bedford	Bedford	Dunstable
Bedford	Burnley	Dewsbury	Dunstable	Finedon
Bramley	Cheadle	Dunstable	Horsham	Hereford
Bradford	Colchester	Hartlepool	Isle of Wight	Horsham
Brentford	Congleton	Horsham	Leighton Buzzard	Kettering
Derby	Coppenhall	Hull	Lowestoft	Leighton Buzzard
Dewsbury	Dover	Isle of Wight	Luton	Loughborough
Dunstable	Hereford	Leighton Buzzard	Petworth	Lowestoft
Ecclesall Bierlow	Horsham	Lowestoft	Salisbury	Luton
Edmonton	Knutsford	Luton	Stamford	Petworth
Gloucester	Leamington	Petworth	Stapleton	Salisbury
Hendon	Leominster	Pontypridd	Walsall	Stapleton
Horsham	Lowestoft	Salisbury		
Leighton Buzzard	Melton Mowbray	Sculcoates		
Lowestoft	Petworth	Stamford		
Luton	Radford	Stapleton		
Maidstone	Runcorn	Tewkesbury		
Petworth	Stapleton	Thanet		
Plymouth		Walsall		
Sculcoates				
Stapleton				
Walsall				
Wolverhampton				

Edward P Walls, JP, Tobacco Manufacturer (RG 12 / 1989, ff. 43–44)

Bibliography

Donald F Begley, *Irish Genealogy: A Record Finder* (Heraldic Artists Ltd, 1981).

John M Boreham, *The Census and How to Use it* (Essex Society for Family History, 1982).

C R Chapman, *Pre 1841 Censuses and Population Listings*, 5th edn (Lockin Publishing, 1998).

Frederick Engels, *The Condition of the Working Class in England*, ed. W O Henderson and W H Chaloner, 2nd edn, Chapter III, p. 30 (Basil Blackwell, 1971).

J S W Gibson, *Census Returns 1841–1891 in Microform: A Directory to Local Holdings in Great Britain*, 6th edn (FFHS, 1994).

J S W Gibson, *Marriage, Census and other Indexes for Family Historians,* 8th edn (FFHS, 2000).

J S W Gibson and Colin Chapman, *Census Indexes and Indexing* (FFHS, 1983).

J S W Gibson and M Medlycott, *Local Census Listings 1522–1930, Holdings in the British Isles*, 3rd edn (FFHS, 1997).

Alan Godfrey, *Old Ordnance Survey Maps* (Gateshead, various dates).

Heraldic Artists Ltd, *Handbook on Irish Genealogy* (Heraldic Artists Ltd, 1978).

E J Higgs, *Making Sense of the Census: The Manuscript Returns for England and Wales, 1801–1901* (HMSO, 1989).

E J Higgs, *A Clearer Sense of the Census* (PRO Handbook 28, HMSO, 1996).

Gordon Johnson, *Census Records for Scottish Families* (Association of Scottish Family History Societies, Aberdeen, 1990).

Susan Lumas, *The Basics of The Census Returns of England and Wales* (FFHS, 2002).

George Pelling, *Beginning Your Family History*, 7th edn (FFHS, 1998).

People and Places in the Victorian Census: a review and bibliography of publications based substantially on the manuscript Census Enumerators' Books 1841–1911. Dennis Mills and Carol Pearce (comp) (Institute of British Geographers, Historical Geography Research Series No. 23, November 1989).

Samuel Cluvers, Vinegar, Pickle and Fruit Preserver (RG 12/4403, f. 48)

The Phillimore Atlas and Index of Parish Registers, ed. Cecil R Humphery-Smith, 2nd edn (Phillimore, 1996).

Population of Each County of Great Britain: 1841 (sessional papers I, House of Commons, Vol. II, paper no. 52, 277).

Population Tables I: Numbers of the inhabitants: Vol. I: 1852–1853 (sessional papers, House of Commons, Vol. LXXXV, paper no. 1631).

Population Tables I: Numbers of the inhabitants: Vol. II: 1852–1853 (sessional papers, House of Commons, Vol. LXXXVI, paper no. 1632).

Population Tables I: Numbers and Distribution of the People: 1862 (sessional papers, House of Commons, Vol. L, paper no. 3056).

Population Tables: Area, Houses and Inhabitants: Vol. I, Counties: 1872 (sessional papers, House of Commons, Vol. LXVI, paper no. c.671–I, Part I).

Population Tables: Area, Houses and Inhabitants: Vol. II, Registration or Union Counties: 1872 (sessional papers, House of Commons, Vol. LXVI, paper no. c.676–I, Part II, 1).

Population Tables: Area, Houses and Population: Counties: 1883 (sessional papers, House of Commons, Vol. LXXVIII, paper no. c.3562, 1).

Population Tables: Registration Counties: 1883 (sessional papers, House of Commons, Vol. LXXIX, paper no. c.3563, 1).

Population Tables: Parliamentary Papers 1893–4 (sessional papers, House of Commons, Vol. CVI, paper no. c.7222)

Population Tables: Parliamentary Papers 1904 (sessional papers, House of Commons, Vol. CVIII, paper no. cd.2174

M E Bryant Rosier, *Index to Census Registration Districts*, 6th edn (FFHS, 1999).

Andrew Todd, *Basic Sources for Family History: Back to the early 1880s,* 3rd edn (Bury, Lancs, 1994).

Ray Wiggins, *St Catherine's House Districts* (privately printed, Northwood, no date).

Joesph Chamberlain, Privy Councellor, MP (RG 12 / 2350, f. 99, p. 16)